Igniting the Passion for Life

by Dudley Hall

Published by
Successful Christian Living Ministries
Euless, Texas

Published by Successful Christian Living Ministries
P.O. Box 101, Euless, TX 76039-0101.

Editorial Services provided by Sue Layman, Solution Resources, Inc.
(Euless, TX)

Editorial Assistance by David Hall (Euless, TX)
Cover Design and Text Layout by Greg Steinle (Euless, TX)

ISBN 1-8888946-00-8
Library of Congress Catalog Card Number: 96-068411

Printed in the United States of America.
First Printing: May 1996.

... **God has poured out
His love in our hearts
by the Holy Spirit,
whom He has given us.**

Romans 5:5

Contents

1 ‖ *When Love Is Ignited*

He was thirteen. Until now girls were at best a necessary evil. They were usually smarter. They giggled too much. They always wanted to get into the "boys only" clubs. They wanted to play on the baseball teams, but could never catch a hot grounder. He sneered when older boys began to betray the clan by talking to the girls. And he definitely had no frame of reference for those who dressed up to take a girl out on a date—what a waste of time. THEN something totally unexpected happened. It slipped up on him from some unseen cavern of unexplored space. Just as he was about to open his potato chip bag at the lunch table, *she* walked by...reddish blonde hair, a few well placed freckles, the cutest little upturned nose, and those eyes...like crystal pools reflecting the bluest of skies. His stomach felt as if he had eaten a hard-boiled egg without taking the shell off. His mouth was dry. No words seem to make sense. Suddenly he became aware that his hair was not combed, his breath might be bad and his clothes might not show off his muscular physique. He was totally discombobulated. Who was this creature? What kind of magical powers did she possess? Why was he, an intelligent, together, totally cool future NFL star, acting so strange?

Something had been ignited inside with the force of a blow torch, something that had not previously existed. Whatever this newly-ignited fire was inside, it would make a huge difference in his life. He would never be the same again. Every aspect of his life would be affected by this firey beast. His thinking would change. His behavior would change. His schedule would change. His goals would change.

What was this fire? This power?

Some would shrug, "It's only puppy love." Whatever the true nature of puppy love, we all have to admit that it is very real to the puppy. Those rationalists who would have us believe that life can be reduced to matter and reason, aren't taking this hard-to-define force seriously enough. Love is here to stay. We can try to ignore it. We can explain it away in terms of chemistry. We can define it in terms of evolutionary development. However, we must realize it has enormous power to affect our lives.

THE HIGHEST FORM OF LOVE

We obviously want to get a little deeper in this discussion than the puppy love stage. However, this is a good natural analogy for the study of the highest form of love. God often gives us clues into spiritual dimensions by showing us expressions in the natural. The question that seems to need an answer here is: How is love ignited? Is it dormant in all of us or is it imparted to us by someone? How do we get to participate in it? When we talk about God's love, Scripture gives some instruction that will help us.

> *...God has poured out his love into our hearts by the Holy Spirit, whom he has given us.*
> Romans 5:5

> *Dear friends, let us love one another, for love comes from God. Everyone who loves has been born of God and knows God. . . This is love: not*

that we loved God, but he loved us and sent his Son
as an atoning sacrifice for our sins.

1 John 4:7, 10

Using the analogy of the thirteen-year old boy and the instruction from Scripture, let's attempt a conclusion. Love touches us when a previously unmet, sometimes unspoken, often unknown need is met. There is something so satisfying and fulfilling in that encounter that we want, in some way, to mesh with the source of it. It is often unexpected because we have not taken the time to analyze and define our inner needs crying out for attention. The teenager didn't know he had a need for affirmation from the opposite sex until that need was ignited.

In Luke chapter 19, we read the story of Zachaeus, a man who had tried to give full meaning to his life by making it secure with financial abundance. He had adopted an ethic that allowed his personal injustice to others, because he defined life in terms of material security. There was something inside him however, that was not satisfied by this narrowly defined existence. He was curious about this Jesus who was the center of controversy. Zachaeus wanted to see for himself, even though friends assured him that it was just another religious zealot trying to make a name for his own cause. I speculate here, but because Zachaeus was of short statue, he probably battled with self-doubt. Perhaps he was convinced that, because of his physical statue and his unpopular occupation, he wasn't worth much. Then it happened...Jesus stopped under the very tree which Zachaeus had climbed in order to get a better view. Was it something in Jesus' eyes? The smile? The fact that Jesus knew his name? "I want to go home with you," Jesus said. That was it. A need had been addressed that turned something on inside ole Zack. You know the rest of the story. By the end of the day, Zachaeus had committed to restore all he had unjustly taken and to give half his money to the poor. He had been impacted by Love. His unmet, unspoken, possibly unknown needs, were suddenly met by an encounter with someone who affirmed his worth and offered forgiveness and hope.

FORGIVENESS IS LOVE

Jesus seemed to tie passionate love to a particular need in all humans. As He was eating dinner at a pharisee's house (Luke 7:36-50), a prostitute came in and began washing Jesus' feet with her tears. The pharisee was indignant. He thought to himself that surely Jesus couldn't be a prophet. He obviously wouldn't let such a woman touch Him if He really knew her character. Jesus responded by telling him a story about two men, each of whom owed money to a certain moneylender. One day, the moneylender decided to forgive both debts because neither man had the money to pay him back. One was forgiven approximately $30,000. The other was forgiven $3,000. *"Now which of them will love him more?"* Jesus asked. Simon the pharisee answered correctly, *"I suppose the one who had the bigger debt cancelled."* Jesus concluded the session with, *"Therefore, I tell you, her many sins* (the prostitute) *have been forgiven—for she loved much. But he who has been forgiven little loves little."*

Isn't Jesus relating the prostitute's passionate love response to her experience of forgiveness? A crucial need is met when one is forgiven. This causes the forgiven one to respond with extravagant expressions of adoration and affection. Maybe we have lost the sense of needing to be forgiven with all the focus these days on "feeling good about ourselves." When we face the fact that we need forgiveness and experience genuine forgiveness through Jesus Christ, we find the very thing we need and have been searching for—respect, honor and affirmation in the truest sense. Simon, who sought to impress Jesus with his devotion and purity, did not get to drink of the elixir of "heart touching heart". He demanded respect, honor and affirmation, and received a rebuke for his lack of love. The prostitute who asked for nothing but recognized her need for forgiveness, was honored, respected and affirmed by the Master of devotion and purity.

Why do we avoid forgiveness so strenuously? We avoid it because it presupposes failure on our part. We don't accept sin or failure as a part of our lives. We are fixated on performance. We are still working on the premise that we can please God and fulfill our destiny by perfect performance. This might come as a shock to many of us, but that is no longer an option. Our innocence and the possibility of perfect performance was destroyed by the very first sin in the Garden. The option now is not: perfection/imperfection, but forgiven/unforgiven. To those who still resist the thought that we need to be forgiven, there is a long road of denial, failure and depression ahead. To those who have made peace with their humanity without justifying their fallenness, there is a long journey of being loved and of loving. Beginning this journey of love, however, requires that we recognize our dependence on God and our need for His forgiveness.

We all tend to want some sort of fix. We want to be fixed so that we don't continue to need forgiveness. We are ever on the search for the final solution to our dependence. We try to make our religion perform this miracle for us, and often find ourselves disappointed because it doesn't live up to our expectations. What if God said, "I won't fix you so that you don't fail any more, but I will love you in your failure. I will give you My grace to take your focus off yourself and put it on something much higher." Would you be willing to live with the confidence of being loved, rather than focus on continual self improvement?

Many of us are like the little five-year old girl at the birthday party. She is shy and afraid to participate in the party. In her self-consciousness, she keeps her finger in her mouth and her head bowed low while others try to coax her into the festivities. But she is afraid to get involved because she's a little too self-conscious and unsure of herself—she doesn't feel loved. She will just wait until she gets better, prettier, more mature, bigger. Does that sound at all familiar? We can continue to grieve over our incompleteness, or begin to rejoice in the fact that we are loved— and being loved is as good as it gets. When that reality hits us, we do get better. However, we are not as conscious of the actual improvement as we are the one who met our unmet need.

ASPECTS OF FORGIVENESS

Let's look more carefully at some other aspects of this forgiveness that meets such a gigantic need in us. There are three biblical words that could help us understand the vastness of God's love expressed through the forgiveness offered in Jesus— *reconciliation, redemption and regeneration.*

> *For if, when we were God's enemies, we were reconciled to him through the death of his Son, how much more, having been reconciled, shall we be saved through his life.*
>
> Romans 5:10

Col. 1:19-22
I Cor. 5:18-19

Reconciliation: We didn't know it, but we were enemies of God. There was animosity in us toward God, because man has had rebellion and lawlessness in his heart since the fall of Adam. We have continued to seek ways of giving meaning to life without including God. The futility of that causes much distress. We can't have peace with God or His creation until that animosity is destroyed. When Jesus became a man and paid the penalty of our rebellion, making reconciliation with God a reality, a BIG need was met. And because that need was met, we can actually be friends with God. It is even better than that. We can be as friendly with The Father as Jesus is.

Not based on what we do- on what He did

Redemption: We were not only enemies with God, we were slaves to our selfishness and the master of selfishness, Satan. We were ruled by the forces of the world of darkness.

> *As for you, you were dead in your transgressions and sins, in which you used to live when you followed the ways of this world and of the ruler of the kingdom of the air, the spirit who is now at work in those who are disobedient. All of us also lived among them at one time, gratifying the cravings of our sinful nature and following its desires and*

> *thoughts. Like the rest, we were by nature objects of*
> *wrath.*
>
> <u>Ephesians 2:1-3</u>

Col. 2:13,14

It is no wonder that we had such internal distress. We were slaves and didn't know it. That helps explain our incessant need for respect, affirmation and self-value. We were dehumanized by sin and couldn't break the power of our master. When Jesus bought us out of slavery, He made us sons of God. Now He has given us the riches of His treasure.

Col. 2:13-14   For all things are yours:

> *...whether Paul or Apollos or Cephas or the world*
> *or life or death or the present or the future all are*
> *yours, and you are of Christ, and Christ is of God.* 21 B - 23
>
> <u>1 Corinthians 3:22-23</u>

Our problem now is not our slavery, but our slave-mentality. We find it almost impossible to believe that we have truly been made sons and daughters of God. We hold on to a view of reality that doesn't fully embrace the presence of God's redemptive love in us. In short, we continue to live without the consciousness of His love. As a result, our own capacity to love is limited to human resource—a very limited resource.

Even those who have accumulated vast amounts of Bible knowledge do not necessarily have a grasp on the experience of God's love. We seem to have great difficulty turning what we know about God into the experience of actually knowing Him.

Dr. J.I. Packer suggests how we can make this transition. "The rule for doing this is simple but demanding. It is that we turn each truth that we learn about God into matter for meditation before God, leading to prayer and praise to God." [1]

give examples   Gal 4:4-7

---

[1] **Packer, J.I., <u>Knowing God</u>, (InterVarsity Press, Revised 1993) p. 23.**

Dr. Packer helps us apply this by giving an explanation of meditation. This concept of meditation is essential to the process of the truth becoming the truth we live. Jesus showed us that truth must be lived out, not just understood. "Meditation is the activity of calling to mind, and thinking over, and dwelling on, and applying to oneself, the various things that one knows about the works and ways and purposes and promises of God. It is an activity of holy thought, consciously performed in the presence of God, under the eye of God, by the help of God, as a means of communion with God.

Its purpose is to clear one's mental and spiritual vision of God, and to let His truth make its full and proper impact on one's mind and heart. It is a matter of talking to oneself about God and oneself; it is indeed, often a matter of arguing with oneself, reasoning oneself out of moods of doubt and unbelief into a clear apprehension of God's power and grace." [2]

Regeneration means that we are actually changed. Our essential nature has been affected. We are now indwelt by the Holy Spirit. In fact, we are a new species of man. *"But he who unites himself with the Lord is one with him in spirit."* (I Corinthians 6:17) and *"Therefore, if anyone is in Christ, he is a new creation; the old has gone, the new has come!"* (II Corinthians 5:17). We have not yet received our glorified bodies, so we are left with the "old programming" of the days spent under the prince of this world. But our essence is different. Deep in our inner self, we long to know and please God. That is the nature of the new creation. Our task now is to strengthen and release the inner man to overcome the desires and perspectives of the outer man.

> *You were taught, with regard to your former way of life, to put off your old self, which is being corrupted by its deceitful desires; to be made new*

---

[2] Ibid, p. 23.

in the attitude of your minds; and to put on the new self, created to be like God in true righteousness and holiness.

Ephesians 4:22-24

What a discovery! What a thought! We as believers have the very life of Christ in us. This should generate a spontaneous response of worship and joy to well up in us. If this is what it means to be forgiven, why wouldn't everyone want to experience it?

CONCLUSION

Love is ignited in us when a need is met that we may not have even known about. As sinners, our most basic need is forgiveness. Jesus has met this need by offering God's forgiveness through reconciliation, which cancelled our hostility toward God; through redemption, which broke our bondage to sin's power, and through regeneration, which made us new creations with the desire to know and love God. To know and experience His love, we must not be like the little five-year old girl. We must come out of the corner, take our fingers out of our mouths and embrace the party. We can't be perfect, but we can be forgiven. We can be loved and we can love in response.

> **Father, You know all the needs of my heart—those I feel aren't met, those I hesitate to speak and those I don't yet acknowledge. Help me to realize that these have all been met in Your precious Son, Jesus. Thank You that Your forgiveness is all encompassing and never ending; that You drew me to Yourself through love's reconciling, redemptive and regenerating work. And thank You for igniting the passion within me. In Jesus' Name, Amen.**

2 ‖   *THE SEARCH*
FOR LOVE

"The journey is the goal," he said rather matter-of-factly. "An interesting existential viewpoint," I mused as I walked away. Later I was reflecting on this concept and had to agree that it held some very liberating possibilities. Everyone is on the journey. I call it The Search. Why is the whole of the human race breathlessly looking for something it doesn't have? We, like Solomon, have tried to find it in wisdom, wine, women, work, winning, wondering and whining. Why the search? What are we looking for? Why don't our findings satisfy?

THE SEARCH

Man's perpetual search is an evidence of his former state and a result of the fall of man in Adam. God meant for us to enjoy Him and manage His creation under His rule. To do this, however, would require that we partake in His very life. When we (in Adam) chose to live by the knowledge of good and evil, we were separated from the life of God and began the tortuous task of living independently on the earth. But the longing for "life" is still there. We have desperately tried to find substitutes, but to no avail. Nothing can substitute for life but life. Where is life? What does it look like? How do we get it? Although they may phrase it somewhat differently, these are the questions that all men, everywhere are asking. Let's try to find some answers.

There is good news in history. A second Adam exists, and He made the choice for life instead of independence. That choice made it possible for us to be a part of His new race of people. This Adam is the expression of the heart of the one true God. God was searching through the debris of the world and found you. He valued you so much that He decided to pay whatever price necessary to purchase the whole world just to get you. He did that by sending His own son to die to pay the redemption price for you. Before His death, however, that son lived the "life" of the last Adam in the midst of real people and circumstances. It was and is truly a life that is impossible to defeat; one that would make you want to trade everything to get it. For instance, at age twelve He astounded the teachers of His day with the simple wisdom of knowing He was the Son of God. At His first recorded miracle, Jesus honored His mother without letting her agenda get in-the way of His obedience to His heavenly Father. He handled rejection by His home town without bitterness and refused to be defensive, even when He was accused of being demon-possessed. He faced disease, death, demons and division with the same calm as He did the rising of the sun. He was not moved by criticism or praise. He was so aware of His destiny, He could easily refuse to use the manipulative tools of self-promotion to expand His ministry. Jesus could distinguish His role as the Son of God from the ideas and perceptions of the populace. He refused to be caught in the expectations of the religious leaders who wanted to define His role according to their limited concepts. He also refused to be confined by the perception of His close friends, Mary and Martha, at the death of their brother Lazarus. He lived relaxed in the will of the Father while actively doing His Father's business. He was willing to give the priority of His time to only twelve men, believing they would be the key to the success of His mission. He could sleep in the midst of a storm, and feed the thousands to express the abundant love of the Father He represented. He lived free from strife, fear, guilt, contention and boredom. When He offered any explanation of His life, it was that He "was loved of His Father." When He prayed just prior to His death on the cross, He left no mistake that His actions were a response of love to His Father.

"NOT MY WILL BUT THINE"

Hardly anyone in history has found it easy to criticize the life of Jesus. Even those who believe in some other god like to say, "He was a very good teacher and made the world a better place because of His teaching." At first that seems so tolerant and commendable. But He claimed exclusively that His was the only life which was the full expression of the Father. He actually said that He was The Way, The Truth and The Life, and that no one could get to the Father except through Him. Such a claim is truly astounding and demands a response from us. Either He is a liar, a self-deceived prophet or He is who He claimed to be. He can't be all three. If He is "the Life", then we know where the search must be directed. All the maps that present something else as the treasure are useless. We must find Him.

EXPRESSING HIS LIFE

How is it possible to personally know someone who lived two thousand years ago? Well, you'll be happy to know that His life is eternal. Jesus' life took on the form of man approximately two thousand years ago, but He had existed since the beginning. That life is still around and can be lived today—in us. The historicity of Jesus is important, because it was necessary for Him to become a man in order to redeem mankind from bondage. But His death didn't end His life. His death made it possible for us to be released from the penalty of our sins. His resurrection made it possible for us to know Him today. When the Holy Spirit was given at Pentecost, the availability of Jesus' life became ours if we would receive it by faith.

What a thought! We can actually live a life that displaces the strife that tears at our insides and tarnishes our relationships. We can live above the lust that burns in our minds and frightens us even at our best moments. We don't have to be controlled by fears that take the adventure out of life and reduce us to reactors. We can be free from the covetousness that clutters our lives with things that promise fulfillment but never produce. We can live focused outside ourselves. We do not have to be doomed to navel-gazing and self-evaluation for the rest of our lives. It is possible for I Corinthians 13 to actually be experienced rather than just admired. We have been content to admire the treasure without obtaining it.

> *Love is patient, love is kind. It does not envy, it does not boast, it is not proud. It is not rude, it is not self seeking, it is not easily angered, it keeps no record of wrongs. Love does not delight in evil but rejoices with the truth. It always protects, always trusts, always hopes, always perseveres. Love never fails...And now these three remain: faith, hope and love. But the greatest of these is love.*
>
> 1 Corinthians 13:4-8a, 13

I was visiting some friends who live near the mountains of western Canada. The view from the window was majestic. As I stood there admiring the mountains, I was moved to ask, "When can we go climb them?" "We just want to be close enough to admire them. We don't want to climb," they said. I understood what they meant. There are some things I want to appreciate from a distance. Getting closer will require more energy than I want to expend. But we cannot afford to admire the life of love from afar. It will not be enough to dream about the superiority of this life and write poems about it—we must have it. It is like the treasure in the field.

> *The kingdom of heaven is like treasure hidden in a field. When a man found it, he hid it again, and*

*then in his joy went and sold all he had and bought
that field.*

Matthew 13:44

A GOOD TRADE

The value of the life of Jesus requires that we decide to trade everything in order to get it. It is not a regrettable trade, but a joyful one. In fact, we can't afford not to trade. We can't continue to live trying to eliminate those menacing fears, lusts and barriers that frustrate our lives. We have tried enough of the world's solutions where we always end up thinking about ourselves, trying to overcome our own victimization. We have tried the way of religion and ended up tired; tired of failing to live by the high standards expected of us. We have tried philosophy's solution and ended up confused by the holes left in every system of thought. What do we have left to lose? *This* is what we have to "give up" to get the life of Jesus? And we are fussing about that? Believe me, it's really no loss at all. Who ever penned this list seemed to understand a good trade.

> Indulgence says, "Drink your way out"
> Philosophy says, "Think your way out"
> Science says, "Invent your way out"
> Industry says, "Work your way out"
> Communism says, "Strike your way out"
> Militarism says, "Fight your way out"
> Christ says, "I AM the way out"
> Author Unknown

This concept, that repentance is trading up, is not at all like what I heard as a boy listening to the Sunday sermon. It sounded to me then like I had to give up everything fun in life just to go to heaven. I didn't understand that it was a trade UP. I think some people, including me, have tried to cut a deal. We have tried to get the peace and pleasure of Jesus' life without buying the whole field. We try to hold on to the position of governor of our world, while seeking to access the life of peace. We must face it! To be governed by Jesus is to be governed by Love. That means our lives will be characterized by such qualities as meekness, patience, humility and submission to the will of God. We can't have peace and victory without the presence of these qualities. We know our value system has changed when these qualities replace power, prestige, popularity and the world's peace that we have been seeking.

There is another point we need to clarify. This kind of love comes only from God. Love is not some mystical thing with a definition left to the individual or a consensus of culture. *God is the source.* He is the one who defines love and gives it boundaries. Love is received and will be maintained according to His order, and it will not violate the boundaries He has set for it. In other words, this is not the love that people use to justify all kinds of deviant behavior. All of us have heard the "love justifies anything" morality of human religion. The love that comes from God does not break any of the laws He has given in nature or in Scripture. His kind of love is not natural to natural man; that is, man cannot access this love without relationship with God through Jesus. To experience it, we must come only to Him and buy into His government. The question now is, do you believe His life of love is superior to your life, and are you willing to trade up to get it?

THE HIGHEST VALUE

A picture is worth a thousand words. I believe that. When God opens Heaven for a glimpse at reality, faith is the natural result. Jesus taught His earthly disciples to pray, *"Our Father...Your will be done on earth as it is in heaven"* (Matthew 6:9-10). Obviously, something is going on in heaven. In The Revelation, the Apostle John was allowed to see into heaven (Revelation 1:9-20). He saw everyone worshipping before a throne. That should give us a clue to the nature of God's majesty. When we see Him clearly, we too will worship. In the midst of worship, however, John saw something that greatly troubled him—no one was qualified to open the book with the seven seals. This book contained the keys to knowing reality—past, present and future. One of the elders told John to stop crying, for there was One who could perform this feat. It was the Lion of the tribe of Judah. Yet, when John looked for the Lion on the throne in heaven, instead he saw a Lamb that had been slain. What is this saying to us? In heaven, where God's will is being done without hesitation or perversion, the One who rules the universe is a Lamb who was slain but is alive. Whatever the Lamb represents is the highest value in heaven. Another way of saying it is, where the Kingdom of God is recognized, the qualities of Jesus' life are magnified. What are the qualities of the Lamb? Let me just mention four: *meekness, humility, patience* and *submission* to the will of God.

Contrary to what many think, *meekness* is not synonymous with weakness. Moses was known as the meekest man in the Old Testament. He certainly was not weak. His leadership abilities, when brought under the control of God, were unmatched in several thousand years. He faced down Pharaoh, the most powerful man on earth. He faced the Red Sea. He even faced two million Israelites who grumbled at his leadership. God didn't diminish his strength when He encountered Moses at the burning bush. He simply brought it under control. The simplest picture of meekness for me is the picture of a wild stallion with a bridle and saddle on. His strength is still intact, but he is under the control of another.

Jesus made it very clear to those who witnessed His ministry that He was willingly under the control of The Father. He did nothing of His own initiative. He lived in order to express the nature of His Father.

> *I have brought you glory on earth by completing the work you gave me to do. And now, Father, glorify me in your presence with the glory I had with you before the world began. I have revealed*

*you to those whom you gave me out of the world.
They were yours; you gave them to me and they
have obeyed your word.*

John 17:4-6

Meekness is the key to tapping the resources of God. As long as we are trying to get God to energize our own endeavors, faith doesn't seem to work. When we live to please Him, He provides the resources to get it done.

It was His lamb qualities that caused Jesus to give priority to private prayer. He had to know the will of the Father if He was to be the agent of accomplishing that will. *Patience* gave Him the calmness to wait thirty years, while the world continued to decay, before His ministry started. *Submission* to His Father's agenda allowed Him to heal some people while others were not addressed. He knew He was sent to do the will of God, not to be a popular Messiah figure. *Humility* allowed Him to wash the feet of the disciples; even the one who would betray Him in a few hours. It was His "lambness" that made the cross possible. He stood innocent before the injustice of the religious and civil courts, never offering to defend Himself, all so that He could shed His blood to save us. Can we even comprehend this kind of love?

How strange that God's universe is ruled by a slain Lamb! We use all sorts of animals to represent governments—the bear, the eagle and the tiger. But a lamb? It certainly is a novel idea. To rule by sacrifice??? It is surely strange living to live in a culture where love is power, trust is the highest currency and freedom means the opportunity to serve. But it is living of the highest value.

CONCLUSION

When Jesus came proclaiming the Kingdom of God, hardly anyone understood that He was referring to this kind of living. Do you suppose the reason we have such difficulty in our living is that we have not embraced His definition of life? Is it possible that we have redefined love to fit into our system of values, polluted with self-absorption, and come out with a word void of real meaning? Maybe all this talk about love is just that—talk. What if we really believed that the life of Jesus was available to us today. Wouldn't it be worth the effort to find it and embrace it? Wouldn't that be better use of our time than the elusive search for fame or fortune? Let's take the gamble. Let's sell it all for the hope of real life. If it exists, and if it is "findable", let's find it.

> **I spend a great deal of time searching, Father, when, in fact, I already have the treasure—the life of Jesus. Teach me, Lord, to do more than just admire this treasure; teach me to experience it. Thank You that I don't have to bargain, but that You offer a priceless trade. I love You, Father. Amen**

3 ▌ *I AM LOVED TO LOVE*

Peter could not believe what he was hearing. Jesus had just said that all the disciples were going to forsake Him. "Surely this could never happen," thought Peter; "at least not by me." But as he looked around the group he began thinking, "Maybe Thomas. After all, he seems to have major struggles with his doubts at times. I could see where it would be possible for Thomas to forsake the Lord. And Matthew, of course. His background is against him because he is so accustomed to dealing with money. A person who has tasted riches has a hard time giving it all up in the final say so. Yes, I can see where Matthew might fall away. And what about John? I know John loves the Lord, but he is awfully soft. He is very tender and sensitive. When things get tough, he could possibly fall away. Then there is Nathaniel. He has always had some philosophical questions about Jesus. I can see him falling away. But *I* would never do that. Nothing could make me forsake the Lord."

THE SERVANT'S SERVICE

The Apostle Peter was expressing the kind of attitude that

reveals he was not aware of his own dirty feet. In Jesus' last few hours with the disciples, He chose to express His final act of love to them as a group by washing their feet (John 13:1-17). Needless to say, none of the disciples, including Peter, had a clue as to the depth of the meaning of this act of love by Jesus. Jesus was not only doing something very practical for them—washing their feet so they wouldn't soil the linen around the table where they were eating, but He was also providing for them a model of how His Life should be expressed through them from that point on. It was also a model for how they should treat one another with the love He was about to impart to them through His death, burial and resurrection.

It might help us to review a little about the culture of those days. People usually traveled by foot. The unpaved roads were covered with dust and the dung from animals that pulled the carts which were used as a major mode of transportation. It was common for people's feet to be soiled when they reached someone's house. And it was customary that a servant would wash the feet of those entering the house. As the disciples gathered around for a meal, they would recline on pillows. This style of seating caused the head of one to be very close to the feet of another. So you can see the importance of their feet being clean. What Jesus was about to do for His disciples was not some unheard of act of service. It was something that happened almost every time people came into a house. However, it was never done by the master of the house. It was seen as a menial task, typically done by some unskilled servant. When Jesus surprised all the disciples by getting up, girding Himself with the towel and picking up the basin, He was revealing to them the very heart of the Father. He was showing that, from the beginning, it was in God's heart to condescend to our level to meet our needs.

> *Your attitude should be the same as that of Christ Jesus: who,being in the very nature of God,did not consider equality with God something to be grasped but made himself nothing, taking the very*

*nature of a servant being made in human likeness.
And being found in appearance as a man, he
humbled himself and became obedient to death
even the death on the cross! There God exalted him
to the highest place and gave him the name that is
above every name, that at the name of Jesus every
knee should bow in heaven and on earth and under
the earth and every tongue confess that Jesus
Christ is Lord to the glory of God the Father.*

Philippians 2:5-11

It has always been God's mode of operation to come to man's level to reveal Himself to us. It was true when God came and spoke to Abraham and made a covenant with him. Remember, it was not Abraham who was seeking for God, but God sought Abraham and initiated the covenant. Later it was God who came and picked Moses to lead His children out of bondage. It was God who told Moses to meet Him in the mountain so that He, God, could give Moses the ten commandments. It was God who chose to become a man in the person of Jesus Christ so that we could finally understand and relate to Him. And now Jesus was again modeling for the disciples the very nature of the Father. He was also previewing His coming death, something they would not understand until much later. He wanted them to know that the essence of their ministry was not in skills but in the attitude of service.

RECEIVE TO GIVE

Maybe the most important thing we are supposed to learn out of this servanthood passage of John chapter 13, is that we can only give away a love that we have first received from God Himself. To try and emulate His actions without first being a recipient of His love is arrogance and foolishness. A life of true freedom in ministry is the life that has been touched by unconditional love and then released to give that love away. The poison of pseudo-Christian religion is the attempt to try to model a life of ministry after Jesus without humbling oneself to have his feet washed by the Master.

Like Peter, we still have obstacles to receiving this ministry of love. To have our feet washed by the Master is uncomfortable. It also produces a severe case of self-consciousness. If you have ever had someone offer to wash your feet, you know the uncomfortable feeling of submitting to their act of service. All of a sudden you are conscious that your toes are large or have callouses. You are hoping your socks don't have holes in them. Everything within you is wanting to say, "Thank you very much for the offer, but really, I can do without it." Maybe this type of experience helps us understand Peter's refusal when Jesus came to him in the rotation and was about to wash his feet. Peter knew who was making the offer. This was *"the Christ, the Son of the Living God"* (Matthew 16:16). It just was not right for Him to be kneeling beneath them washing their feet. On this occasion Jesus made it very clear to Peter (and subsequently to us) that He was doing more that washing some dust particles from Peter's fleshly feet. He was demonstrating the necessity of their (and our) total dependence upon Him to wash away the daily defilement of worldly sins from our lives. If we neglect this essential, we will truly have *"no part with him."* God never intended to fix us to the extent that we would not daily need Him for our cleansing and equipping. We, like Peter, have allowed our discomfort in being humbled to make excuses for hanging on to our defilement. We have either chosen to continue living with defiled feet as we stumble along, or we have sought to wash our own feet. We feel this way because we are ashamed that our feet are dirty. Actually, there is no shame involved in getting your feet dirty when you are walking in a dusty world. This is true physically or spiritually. The dust of the lust of the flesh, the lust of the eye and the pride of life will attach itself to even the purest of Christians as he walks in the world. Therefore, we need the constant application of the blood of Jesus to cleanse us from all our guilt of unrighteousness. Our obsession with perfection will prohibit our taking the essential cleansing that keeps us continually dependent upon our intercessor, Jesus Christ.

CONTINUAL CLEANSING

Peter was not aware that in a few days he would need this cleansing all over again. However, it was out by the Sea of Galilee after Peter's betrayal of Jesus, after the crucifixion and resurrection, that Jesus washed Peter's spiritual feet. As they sat by the breakfast fire Jesus said, *"Do you love me?...Feed my sheep"* (John 21:15-17). Here again we find the aggressive unconditional love of the Master washing away the defilement of Peter's failure in his greatest point of testing. This was not the last time Peter would need the ministry of the towel and basin from the Lord. Often in his imperfect life he needed to sit while the Master of the universe knelt at his feet and washed away the defilement of the world.

We should note that if this was true for one of Jesus' chief disciples, it will certainly be true for us. We must get accustomed to receiving that which we do not deserve and cannot earn. We will all agree that "it is just not right" for Jesus to kneel beneath us and wash our feet. And yet that and that alone is what cleanses us from the defilements that would destroy our lives. We can neither make up for our mistakes nor can we totally prevent them. What we can do, is receive His unmerited love and rejoice in that love.

The second major obstacle to receiving Jesus' ministry of love was also voiced for us by Peter. He went from neglecting the essential to clamoring for the unnecessary. When Jesus told Peter that unless He washed Peter's feet he would have no part in Jesus, Peter replied *"Wash not only my feet but my whole body."* Jesus mildly rebuked Peter by saying essentially, "If you have had a bath you don't need to be washed all over, only that part which is defiled." History shows this has continually been one of the major obstacles in living out the Christian experience. We seem to want to redo the bath when all that is needed is the footwashing. In once sense, this is a depreciation of what we have received in our permanent relationship with Christ. To try to overcome the confusion of our defilement, we have sought to go back and redo our justification. Many precious believers have endured doubt for a long time and sought to remove it by going back and "being saved all over again." It is true that many people have accepted a substitute in place of a personal relationship with Jesus Christ. They need to genuinely go back and meet Him initially as their personal Savior. However, a great number of believers find themselves continually starting all over again because of what they believe to be a defective relationship.

At this writing, my wife and I have been married for twenty-seven years. During that time there have been some interesting challenges and bumps in our fellowship. Never once have we concluded that our problems were because we did not do the ceremony right. What we have had to face each time was a defilement in the relationship, and that defilement had to be faced then. There is a major need for modern-day Christians to appreciate what we already have. *"Only let us live up to what we have already attained."* (Philippians 3:16)

We were bathed completely when we were given a *by-faith righteousness* in Jesus Christ. We no longer have to struggle with our own inability to live up to God's standards. Jesus came and lived in our place. He lived up to all the standards that God requires for man. When we come into Him by faith, all of His performance is credited to our account, and all our failure—past, present and future—is paid for through His death. If we are in a position of trusting Him, then we stand before God as righteous as Jesus Christ. This does not need to be redone; it needs to be lived out. Not only do we have a by-faith righteousness, but our "bath" also included an authority given to us in the name of Jesus.

> *In that day you will no longer ask me anything. I tell you the truth, my Father will give you whatever you ask in my name. Until now you have not asked for anything in my name. Ask and you will receive*

and your joy will be complete.

John 16:23-24

Again, this is not something we merit by our performance, but rather, it is a gift from God. But it is a gift that is to be used; otherwise, it benefits us nothing. In fact, when we don't use a gift that has been given to us, we insult the giver. When the defilement of the world settles on our feet and begins to cause disruption in our fellowship and distraction in our ministry, we don't have to go back and get the whole bath anymore. However, we do need to use our authority in prayer by asking for and receiving the cleansing from our defilement. That authority, however, is not limited to our receiving cleansing but is imparted to us to perform the ministry that Jesus did while He was on the earth. We now have the privilege of extending the impact of the Kingdom of God through our lives as we use the name of Jesus in authoritative praying.

Another wonderful aspect of our bath is the gift of the Holy Spirit who lives within us. *"Do you not know that your body is the temple of the Holy Spirit, who is in you, whom you have received from God? You are not your own."* (I Corinthians 6:19) Our continual clamor for new experiences as we seek to deal with the inconsistencies in our lives, shows that we have not learned to appreciate what we have in experiencing the daily cleansing of the Lord's love. We need the exhortation in Hebrews chapter 6.

> *Therefore let us leave the elementary teachings about Christ and go on to maturity, not laying again the foundation of repentance from acts that lead to death and of faith in God, instructions about baptisms, the laying on of hands, the resurrection of the dead, and eternal judgment.*
>
> Hebrews 6:1-2

THE MINISTRY OF LOVE

Earlier we said that Jesus washed the disciples feet to show the necessity of our submitting to His continual love and as a model of what disciples are to do for each other for the rest of their lives. The inevitable result of receiving the ministry of the towel and basin, is that it motivates our inner man to give that same ministry to one another. It is interesting to note that, though Jesus said this is what we are to do for each other, we don't find Christians in the book of Acts spending a lot of time washing one another's physical feet. However, we do find them taking the lesson they learned here and practicing the ministry of the towel and basin in spiritual applications.

I want to mention four ways that modern disciples can wash one another's feet: *honor, encouragement, intercessory prayer* and *generosity.*

Honor: We can help wash away the envy that gets on our brothers as they walk in this world. It is almost inevitable to be tainted by envy because we live in a society where it is such a major component. Instead of standing off and criticizing each other for getting dirty, the ministry of the towel and basin would encourage us to wash away the envy by honoring one another. We can honor one another by recognizing each other's gifts and unique place in the body of Christ. The Apostle Paul did this very well when he wrote to his friend in the epistles, calling them by name and mentioning their contributions to the work in the Kingdom. *"I commend you to our sister Phoebe, a servant of the church in Cenchrea . ... Greet Priscilla and Acquilla, my fellow workers in Christ Jesus. They risked their lives for me. ... Greet my dear friend, Epenetus, who was the first convert to Christ in the providence of Asia...Greet Mary, who worked very hard for you."* (Romans 16:1,3-4a,5b-6)

Most sincere Christians have a keen sense of their own failure. They don't need brothers and sisters-in-Christ pointing out their failures as much as they need us honoring them for their efforts to bring glory to Christ and advance the cause of the Kingdom.

Encouragement: It is impossible for our brothers to walk in the cynical world without getting some of the dust of criticism on them. Criticism, whether justified or not, hurts and often times paralyzes. Christians who join in criticizing one another not only help disable a brother, but actually become a part of the company of the accuser of the brethren. We can help wash away this criticism by our words and actions of encouragement. I have yet to meet a person who has had too much encouragement. I can honestly say no one has ever said to me, "Please don't encourage me anymore, I have had more than I can stand." We could learn a lot from our Lord here; as He related to people, He focused on their destiny rather than their history. It was true when Jesus first met Peter. Jesus knew that Peter had some rough spots and would need quite a bit of adjusting. Yet, He saw Peter's destiny and told him his name and character would be that of a rock—even when, at that time, it was more akin to a mud ball.

We find a similar story in the Old Testament as the angel of the Lord appeared to Gideon. Gideon was hiding behind a wine press seeking to thresh out enough grain for lunch, when the angel of the Lord said to him, *"The Lord is with you, mighty warrior"* (Judges 6:12). Gideon felt sure whoever had said that made a big mistake. Gideon was anything but a mighty warrior. He felt like a scared child. Yet, it was this word of encouragement spoken to him by the Lord Himself that ignited a fire in Gideon to become the leader of the small army that routed the Midianites.

I have known some Christians to get upset when a positive prophecy was given about a brother in whom there was known inconsistencies. It seems as though we want people to be exposed and chastised. Yet God's word of encouragement is aimed at the inner man, seeking to build up the inner man so the outer man can be conquered.

Intercessory Prayer: The dust of discouragement seems to be on every street of our journey. Fellow believers need their feet washed from this terrible defilement. This can be done in many ways but primarily through a ministry of intercessory prayer. We can always lift each other up in prayer, especially when there is nothing else we can do. Remember, we have been given the authority of Jesus' name. And the Father has promised to answer our prayers that are asked in His name so that our joy is complete and He is glorified. When we find a fellow traveler whose toes are caked with the discouragement of the world, let's get out the towel and basin of prayer and wash their feet.

Generosity: We live in a culture permeated with materialism and greed. These ugly lusts continually attach themselves to our lives, and we find ourselves wanting things for the strangest of reasons. While our tendency is only to rebuke, it would be a better idea to express generosity. Generosity has a way of exposing greed in its essence and liberating those who are in its clutches. Using our gifts of hospitality and the liberality of giving, we can help each other make it through a materialistic world.

These are only four suggestions. I am sure you could think of many more. I am also sure that if you allow Jesus to wash the defilement from your life daily, there will be something inside of you that wants to wash it from the lives of others.

CONCLUSION

The natural tendency for all of us, like Peter, is to reject the essential of submitting to the Lord's ministry of love. It is uncomfortable and humiliating to admit that we, as mere humans, must allow Jesus to wash our feet. It would be much easier if there were some way we could do it ourselves or if we could prevent them from getting dirty in the first place. The next problem is that we depreciate the wonderful benefits of being in Christ Jesus by seeking to redo our relationship instead of living out the benefits that are already ours by faith.

In New Testament times, each teacher had an emphasis that would mark His disciples as distinctive. Jesus said that the mark He chose to put on His disciples was basically this, "They will know you are my disciples by how you love one another." I don't think He has changed His distinctiveness. It is the same today. The world will know we are disciples of Jesus if we love like He loves. The only way we can accomplish that is by receiving daily doses of His unconditional, unmerited love and then passing it on to the "brothers and sisters" as we have opportunity.

Thank you, Father, for showing me that servanthood is really love in action, and that I can only give it away after I have first received it from You. Thank You that Your love cleanses me continually. I humble myself before You, Father, that I may honor You and others. In Jesus' Name, Amen.

4 ‖ SAFE IN THE ARMS OF LOVE

The two men were discussing the benefits and casualties of a life of service. One finally said, "For every Mother Teresa that is noticed by the world and given recognition, there are hundreds of forgotten ministers and missionaries who are thrown on the garbage heaps of life because they did not learn life's most important lesson, *You must look out for number one* ."

KNOWING OUR PURPOSE

How do you get ready to live a life of service? What are the guarantees that if you give your life away, you will not be taken advantage of? How could Jesus, with genuine joy, serve His disciples knowing that all would forsake Him, one would deny Him and one would betray Him? We must be reminded that Jesus was living His life as a man in total dependence upon the Father. This should give us encouragement as people of faith. We too can get beyond our self-centered agendas and self-conscious awareness to a place where we genuinely "lose our lives for His sake."

Jesus knew that the Father had put all things under

His power and that He had come from God and was returning to God; so He got up from the meal took off his outer clothing and wrapped a towel around His waist. After that, He poured water into a basin and began to wash the disciples feet, drying them with the towel that was wrapped around Him.

John 13:3-5

In short, Jesus knew where He had come from, where He was going, and what resources had been granted to Him by the Father. These are the essential ingredients to prepare us for the enchanting life of love.

We must have a sense of our own personal divine history. As surely as Jesus came from God, we too have the assurance that we were created by God, in His image and with a purpose. In contrast to the view of the naturalist, who insists that we are a product of time plus matter plus chance, we have chosen to believe God's explanation of the origin of things. We have declared, in agreement with Him, that we are creations rather than accidents.

For you created my inmost being, you knit me together in my mother's womb. I praise you because I am fearfully and wonderfully made; your works are wonderful, I know that full well. My frame was not hidden from you when I was made in the secret place. When I was woven together in the depths of the earth, your eyes saw my unformed body...

Psalms 139:13-16a

Much of the lack of purpose prevalent in modern society, is the result of man's refusal to believe that he has a divine origin. When we accept as valid the naturalist's assumption that matter is all that exists, then we subtract God's creative purposes from the equation of reality, and we inevitably wind up with a philosophy of absurdity. Christians have chosen to believe that God is not only behind history and that He is the prime mover of all things, but that He is actively involved in history.

Since this is true, then we have every reason to believe we have a design and a purpose—a purpose that can be known. In fact, God is actively involved in helping us find and fulfill that purpose. History has value and meaning because it tells the story of an active God bringing things to a specified end. God's created design has not been thwarted. No slip ups nor mistakes have destroyed His plan. Therefore, we can live at peace with our frame. God has not put a single painting in the wrong frame. Even our bodies provide a clue to our purpose and give us a sense of self-respect and honor. The cultural models placed before us to emulate, seek to create a dissatisfaction with who we are. Every young girl that does not have the perfect "model" figure feels in some way insignificant and less valuable. Every young man who does not fit the mold of the perfect "male specimen" also fights the same battle. Many of us have wondered how a God of love could have made us so "uncool".

The part in the middle of my hair began to expand a few years ago until now my center part is quite wide. I am amazed at how many people like to make jokes about bald people. They are trying to convince us that baldness is not the norm. I, along with some other shiny heads, have decided to believe that we are the norm and that some others are just extremely hairy. I have been amazed through the years how many people would ask me, "Does it bother you being bald?" My usual answer is, "Do I have a choice?" I decided a long time ago to make peace with my broad part and my big ears. Admittedly, I would not have drawn it up that way had I been the creator. But evidently He knew something I didn't. I am willing to accept the frame He has put me in as the right one. After all, He is the Master Artist.

Because we believe God controls our history, we can make peace with our family. Many people recount how, as children, they wished they belonged to another family. With all the dysfunctional families that are in existence, this should hardly come as a surprise. What is a surprise however, is that this seems to have been the case even with many who had very happy families. We tend to compare our known problems with other people's unknown ones. Our placement in our specific family was an act of God. This too can become a clue to our identity and destiny. If you had lived in Old Testament times and were born into the Levite family, you had a giant clue as to what you would spend your life doing. Though the strict limitations to the Levites are not given to all of us, we are foolish not to look at the values and the ramifications of our family relationships in helping us discover essentially who we are. We have too often bought into the lie that to discover our true identity, we must separate ourselves from our history and our family, and find ourselves through an existential choice that is somehow supposed to create meaning out of nothing.

My call to the ministry was mixed with confusion about this very idea. I was born into the home of a farmer. I was the fifth of five children and had a very happy, normal home life. My brother, who was sixteen years older than I, had been called into the ministry. He was the first in our family that we could remember making this choice. In my late teens, when I was trying to decide what my vocation would be, I quickly eliminated the ministry. I determined that considering the ministry had to be a subconscious motive to follow my older brother. I felt sure the community would say I just wanted to be like my brother. After many months of unnecessary struggle, I came to a conclusion. Regardless of what the community might say, and disregarding my inability to discern my own motives, I decided to follow what I believed to be the voice of God and enter the ministry. I later discovered that God was directly involved in placing me in a family with an older brother who had blazed a path which would make my path even easier. Instead of my family being a hindrance to discovering my identity, it actually became a help.

But someone may raise the objection that their family was not a healthy, normal one. How would they be able to get a clue about their destiny from a dysfunctional family? The answer just may lie in one word—"overcomer". God has designed us so that we exhibit the nature of His life, which is an overcoming life. Therefore, even early on, we are given obstacles to overcome that teach us to turn to Him and rely on Him. The body we are given or the family we are placed in are often obstacles that we overcome, and in overcoming we discover more of the nature of God.

Before we leave this discussion about our divine history, let me mention one other aspect. To believe that God controls our history, gives us the grace to make peace with our own generation. God has not made any mistakes in where He has placed us in time. My place in my generation will help me discover the message and the method that I am to use in participating in the Father's business. My being born in the late forties, has made me part of one of the most influential segments of society that has ever existed in the United States. I am a baby boomer. The baby boomers have determined for several decades the approach to marketing for our whole society. Personally, I am tired of hearing about baby boomers. But I have made peace with the fact that I was born at the right time. That helps me understand my place in history as I seek to prepare the next generation to live beyond the temporal materialism and selfish confines of baby boomerism.

KNOWING OUR POSITION

Jesus not only knew where He came from, but He knew that His resources were given to Him by the Father. The wonderful news here is, because of our relationship with Christ Jesus, we too have been given the same kind of resources. We too have authority and power. All Christians need to understand two phrases which describe this authority and power. The two phrases are; "in Christ" and "Christ in you." The phrase "in Christ" tells us of our position before God. Accepting our position determines our perspective. It is important that we see everything from our position of inclusion in Jesus Christ. Ephesians chapter 1 states this truth repeatedly. Notice all the benefits that are ours because of our position in Christ. *"...has blessed us in the heavenly realms with every spiritual blessing in Christ...He chose us in Him before the creation of the world...In Him we have redemption through His blood, the forgiveness of sins...Having believed, you were marked in Him with a seal, the promised Holy Spirit,..."* (Ephesians 1:3-4,7,13)

To help explain this concept, let me share the illustration of the barrel. If I took you today and placed you inside a barrel and threw the barrel into the river, where would you be? Obviously you would be in the river. Why? You would be in the river for one reason; because of your relationship to the barrel. You are in the barrel and the barrel is in the river. Therefore, you are in the river. If I then took the barrel and put it in the White House, behind the President's desk, where would you be? You would be seated in a place of authority. Why? There is just one reason; because of your relationship to the barrel. You are in the barrel and the barrel has been placed there. It is a crude illustration, but shows that our position before God is not the result of something *we* have done, but because of someone (Jesus) to whom we are related.

Because Jesus Christ died and we are in Him, we died. Because He was buried and we are in Him, we were buried. Because He was raised from the dead and we are in Him, we were raised from the dead and have resurrection life. Because the Father took Him to heaven and seated Him at the right hand of God's authority, that too is our position—thus our perspective. To evaluate life properly, we must evaluate life from the perspective of our true position in Christ. This will eliminate much of the "poor me" mentality of the Christian experience. We are not victims in this world subject to the whims of the devil and the forces of the principalities and powers. We are, in fact, granted the resources of Jesus' position and are expected to use those resources by faith.

CHRIST'S AVAILABLE POWER

The second phrase we need to understand is "Christ in You." This phrase does not speak so much about our position and perspective as it does about the power that is available to us, as believers, through the indwelling of Christ's life. Paul gives us a clue about that power when he prays for believers in Ephesians chapter 1. Here is a part of his prayer;

> *I pray that the eyes of your heart may be enlightened in order that you may know the hope to which he has called you, the riches of his glorious inheritance in the saints, and his incomparable great power for us who believe. That power is like the working of his mighty strength which he exerted in Christ when he raised him from the dead and seated him at his right hand in the heavenly realms far above all rule and authority, power, and dominion and every title that can be given, not only in the present age but also in the one to come.*
>
> Ephesians 1:18-21

These are great riches mentioned here. However, riches that are not accessed cannot be used. We will live without authority or power unless we access the riches found in these two great realities.

Jesus was able to live the superior life because He believed in His relationship with the Father. Here is His explanation;

> *Don't you believe that I am in the Father and that the Father is in me. The words that I say to you are not just my own, rather it is the Father living in me who is doing His work. Believe me when I say I am in the Father and the Father in me, or else at least believe on the evidence of the miracles themselves.*
>
> John 14:10-11

He was subject to all the pressures that are common to other humans. And we can be sure that many days He did not feel as powerful as He was.

KNOWING OUR DESTINY

A man the Church has known as Brother Lawrence, was a saint who taught many believers how to access the "Christ in us" and to live with a continual consciousness of the presence of God. Listen to his testimony. "For the first year I spent much of the time set apart for devotions thinking about death, judgment, hell, heaven and my sins. I continued this for a few years, applying my mind to these thoughts in the morning and then spending the rest of the day, even in the midst of my work, in the presence of God. I considered that He was always with me, that He was even within me. After a while, I accidentally began doing the same thing in my set time of devotions that I had been doing the rest of the day. This produced great delight and consolation. This practice produced in me so high an esteem for God that faith alone was enough to satisfy all my needs." [3]

Next we come to one of the most profound thoughts that Scripture gives us. Jesus' life was so superior because He not only knew He had come from the Father, and that authority and power had been given to Him, but He also knew why He was sent and where He was going. In short, He knew His destiny. Today there is much discussion about our destiny. It seems we are all looking for that "place in the sun" that will satisfy all our longings for significance and purpose. Many best selling books are written on the topic of how to find our particular place in life, and how to achieve our destiny by discovering the hidden potential within the human species. It is very interesting that when Jesus spoke of where He was going, He did not speak of it in terms of a place, but

---

[3] Brother Lawrence, <u>Devotional Classics,</u> (edited by Foster, Richard and Smith, James Bryan) p. 83.

rather in terms of a person. He was going to the Father. Notice that earlier He said He had come from the Father. You get the impression that Jesus' total focus was on the Father. He had come to the earth and found His destiny in "glorifying" the Father; that is, He had come to reflect all the attention and praise toward the Father. He had come to show humanity what God the Father looked like, how He thought, how He acted and how He responded. Jesus had continually reminded the disciples that He did nothing on His own initiative, but rather as a response to the Father. At one point, He reminded Philip and the other disciples that if they had seen Him they had seen the Father. Jesus was revealing, through His words and actions, one of the most important truths we can ever embrace: THE HIGHEST PURPOSE FOR ANY PERSON IS TO EXALT ANOTHER. THE HIGHEST 'ANOTHER' IS GOD.

GLORIFYING HIM

Why would God create us with the designed purpose to exalt Him? Is that not selfishness on His part? It is obviously not selfishness if God knows that the highest form of happiness and the greatest sense of fulfillment comes when we live our lives to glorify someone else, namely Him. We should have gotten a clue from the very Godhead. We are told on many occasions that Jesus came to exalt the Father, the Father was exalting the Son, and that the Holy Spirit would be sent to exalt the Son who was exalting the Father. In the very community of the Godhead, we find an example of the highest form of life; that is, glorifying another. Jesus Himself gave us a very clear description of this in John chapter 12.

> *Jesus replied, "The hour has come for the Son of Man to be glorified. I tell you the truth, unless a kernel of wheat falls to the ground and dies, it remains only a single seed. But if it dies, it produces many seeds. A man who loves his life will lose it. While a man who hates his life in this world*

will keep it for eternal life. Whoever serves me must follow me; and where I am, my servant will also be. My Father will honor the one who serves me."

John 12:23-26

What is Jesus saying? He is saying that the highest destiny of man is like a seed that falls to the earth and gives up its own independent life so that another life can be expressed through it. How have we missed this so completely? Every seed we see should remind us that our destiny is tied up in yielding our independence so that His life can be manifested in us. ·We are all seeds, and if we choose to maintain our rights and struggle for our own independent destiny, we will miss out on what glory really is. It is only when we are willing to spend our lives for the sake of God's glory that we will even begin to taste the life of love that Jesus lived. It is no wonder that Jesus was anxious to get back to the Father, because all His time on earth was spent magnifying the Father and reflecting everyone's attention back to Him.

We have used the words, but I am not sure we have embraced the reality. We have often said that the chief end of man is to glorify God, yet it seems we are continually trying to find our sense of fulfillment without giving up our own lives for the purpose of expressing His. Living our lives to please Him and draw all attention to Him would free us from our own self-consciousness and shame. This is a necessary ingredient for anyone who is to spend his life in the ministry of divine love. We must embrace our destiny, which is to glorify God. That is where we are going, and if there is anything in us that can make heaven sweeter, it would be to get a head start by glorifying Him while we are still on earth. We know that is exactly what is going on in heaven. In fact, as we read about the scenes in heaven, God is so gloriously good that even John in The Revelation is unable to express His character. John spends more time describing those who are seeing and worshipping God, than he does expressing God's character. Therefore, our view is a picture of people who are seeing this majestic goodness of the Father and are spending the rest of eternity glorifying Him. He has given us the privilege of getting an early start, and we can start now by choosing, as our very own, the destiny God has set for us.

CONCLUSION

We are ready to begin a life of unexplainable love when we know we have been sent by the Father and have made peace with our history. We were created by Him, in His image, with a purpose that He is actively helping us to discover and fulfill. He has placed us "in Christ", and has placed "Christ in us" through His Holy Spirit. We have the resources given to us by the Father, not only to appreciate but also to appropriate. Our destiny is to glorify Him. With this essential knowledge in our minds and embraced with our hearts, we too can live a life of superior love.

Father, you have created a "safe place" for me. In that place, I can know my purpose, my position and my destiny. Thank you that my safe place is "in Christ", and that my resulting power is "Christ in me." Let my life glorify you in all I do, Lord. In Jesus' Name, Amen.

5 ‖ *WHEN LOVE COOLS*

It had only been a few months since Keith's conversion. Now some of the *mature* Christians were asking him to calm down a little. He had a difficult time understanding their caution. He was overwhelmed by the fact that God loved him so much that He had sought him, found him in his confusion and brought him such a wonderful life of peace and excitement. But in the ensuing months he found that Bible study had grown a little laborious. The irritations in others had become more obvious. In fact, his religious life was becoming one of dull duty rather than passionate zeal.

This description is not unlike many who profess to be Christians in Western society. In fact, many polls reveal that as many as 85% of Americans believe in God. Yet the symptoms of boredom are more prevalent than ever. We continue to invent escape routes from our boredom. Drug abuse, the addiction to all types of entertainment and recreation, lawlessness and irresponsibility are all symptoms of people searching for more excitement—more passion in life.

The sad testimony of many is that they don't attend church

because church is dull. Many have gone on to conclude that because church is dull, God must be dull. GOD, DULL? How could the One who knows all the mysteries of the universe and who, in fact, made the universe be dull? We would have to read the New Testament with blinders on to believe that Jesus lived a dull life. And His life was the very expression of the Father. Could we possibly think that walking on the water, calming the storm, raising the dead, healing the sick, turning water into wine and confronting the authorities of the day would be a dull existence? The sad truth is, because many of us have accepted a poor substitute for the life of Jesus, we are experiencing a lukewarm love.

Lukewarm love is a life on the precipice of destruction. When the fire is not hot inside the human soul, there is not enough motivation to truly engage the difficulties of Christian living. God has never made it a secret that the superior life is a life that overcomes. This means that there will always be something to overcome, but it also means there will always be the resources available to get the job done. However, a call to duty will not be enough motivation to cause a person to engage in the difficulties of miraculous living. In the lukewarm heart there is not enough consciousness of His presence to satisfy our legitimate needs. God has designed us for romance. There is something inside of all of us that craves passionate love. When our heart has grown cold and His presence is not real to us, we begin looking to other resources to meet our legitimate needs. This is when we find ourselves being vulnerable to severe temptation.

When the disciples went with Jesus to the garden prior to His crucifixion, He asked them to watch and pray. But their hearts were dull, and they did not have enough motivation to pray during Jesus' most trying hour. As a result, they fell asleep. I'm afraid this is a picture of many of His disciples today. We find ourselves sleeping during the hour of combat, when eternal issues are being decided, because of our dull perception and our lukewarm love.

MAN'S NEED FOR ROMANCE

Man's need for romance can never be satisfied by his own reason, riches or righteousness. Historically these have been man's substitutes for passionate love. History also proves that none of these will produce what passionate love produces—fulfillment, peace and joy. Man is more than a brain and life is more than a machine; therefore, reason alone will never satisfy him. It is interesting to note that some of the smartest physicists alive, who mock the idea of faith as an integral part of man's existence, are concluding that if there is a God, there is no purpose for Him. They believe that the only hope for man is to find some scientific, technological device to get us off this earth and onto some other planets before total destruction comes. The testimony of these and others should say to us that we can get all our questions answered and yet be incomplete. To reduce man to thought and eliminate the romance is not to exalt him, but debase and ultimately destroy him.

It is also clear that man's life cannot be defined by his possessions. How many testimonies must we hear from empty rich people before we believe this? No one has ever been heard to say on his or her death bed, "I wish I had spent more time at the office and more time making money." Yet many have been heard to say at the close of their life, "I wish I had spent more time in my relationships and not wasted so much time accumulating things."

In addition, man's attempts at righteousness, through his efforts to appease God, are a pitiful substitute for life. This will be a greater temptation for most people reading this book than either reason and riches. In fact, worldwide, the greatest substitute for the life of love has been a life of religion. Maybe we should take some time to delve into this. False religion might best be understood in the Genesis story of Cain and Abel. God had required both sons of Adam and Eve to come before Him in worship. Abel came and sacrificed a lamb to the Lord, which pleased the Lord. Cain, on the other hand, brought an offering of the grain and vegetables of the field, which was not pleasing to God. The point here is that God had obviously required a blood sacrifice, and Cain had chosen to try to relate to God on his own terms. He, like mankind following him, wanted to get to God his own way. Cain was exhibiting the fruit of the tree of the knowledge of good and evil. The temptation to Eve and Adam had been that, if they would disobey God, they would know what God knows, and thus could make their own decisions. And, in doing this, they could in fact, be like God. To "be like God" is really the motivation for all false religion. At first it sounds so right that we would want to be God like. Yet, if we examine that motive, it may not be so pure after all. Who wouldn't want to be like God if God is in a position of superiority and respect, if He has all knowledge of all things and has no need to ask anyone anything? If He is complete and independent with all resources at His disposal, then it sounds like a pretty good place to be. All the man-made religions of history point to the fact that man has attempted to get some part of this God nature. The human mind has been ever so creative in finding sacrifices and offerings to try to reach this state of divinity.

FALSE RELIGION

In Matthew chapter 23, Jesus addresses false religion with its symptoms and effects.

Universal Symptoms of False Religion:

o   Deception
o   Idealistic Expectations
o   Man Consciousness
o   The Need for Position

Deception: When we reject God as God, our minds are immediately turned over to believing some kind of lie. Jesus illustrated this earlier in His teachings when He taught about the soil, the sower and the seed in Matthew 13:3-23. He said that when the word is sown in a heart that does not receive it, the devil plucks it away. When the truth is plucked away, the mind is left to receive the substitute seed which is the word of Satan himself. This truth is also reiterated by the Apostle Paul in Romans 1:21, *"For although they knew God, they neither glorified him as God nor gave thanks to him, but their thinking became futile and their foolish hearts were darkened."*

The Pharisees and the Sadducees, who were the epitome of false religion in Jesus' day, were being addressed by Jesus in Matthew 23. Their deception was about their authority and place. Jesus says so succinctly about them, they *"...sit in Moses' seat.....do not do as they do"* (Matthew 23:2-3). In longing for this position of superiority to be like God, they had manipulated for themselves a place of respect and authority. It doesn't take much discernment today to find those of us who are still attempting the same scheme. The religious landscape is scattered with those who have sought to gain their inheritance too early and have tried to make a place for themselves in religious service, when in fact, they have not been qualified by the Lord Himself.

Idealistic expectations: In Matthew 23:4, Jesus talks about the religious leaders of that day placing heavy burdens on the people which the leaders themselves could not do. There is a tendency for all of us to proclaim a higher standard than any of us can reach. The dead give away is our statements of, *"If only..."*. *If only* I were more mature. *If only* I had better teaching. *If only* I understood the scriptures. *If only* I prayed more. *If only* someone would help me, and so on. These idealistic expectations somehow appeal to our desire to be better and to be like God. But idealism is a weak substitute for holiness. God is not into placing idealistic expectations on us. Rather, He gives us His commands and then releases His grace in us to carry them out. The idealism of false religion creates its own fantasy kingdom where everything is ideal. I'll give you an example. Jesus said if you don't forgive every offense neither will the heavenly Father forgive you. In an effort to help people understand the importance of forgiveness, we sometimes put heavy burdens on them by saying things like, "You must not only forgive a person, but you must then feel more positive toward them than before the offense occurred. Otherwise, you haven't forgiven them." That's a burden man can't bear. Forgiveness is a choice, based on a command of God and made possible by the grace of God which He gives to us freely. However, feelings don't immediately line up with our choices. If we have been hurt deeply, it may take some time for those hurts to be cleansed and healed—though we did, in fact, choose to forgive at some specific point. In reality, there are points in the Christian life where we make choices. From those points, the healing and cleansing process begins as the Word of God works in us. To impose some man-made, idealistic standard is not the way of God.

Man consciousness: Matthew 23:5 says, *"Everything they do is done for men to see; they make their phylacteries wide* (small boxes containing Scripture texts worn for religious purposes) *and the tassels on their garments long."* Phylacteries are no longer in style, at least in Western Christendom. Still, we have all kinds of symbolic phylacteries in our formulas, doctrines and practices. The problem is that any religious fruit we wear on the outside, with the motive to be seen of men, is a dead giveaway that we have bought into a false religious system and have, in fact, been seduced by a religious spirit. If we really want to be free from this bondage, we need to honestly ask and answer these questions; "Is reward my applause? Is rejection my fear?" If we do things for the applause of men or to avoid the rejection of men, then we have accepted a poor substitute for motivation in our behavior. "Professional" Christians find it easy to get caught in the trap of doing religious activities for fear someone might see them not participating and judge that they are unspiritual.

The need for position: Jesus instructed the Pharisees and the religionists of His day not to try to get titles like rabbi, father, master, leader and so forth. Why do men continually grapple for these things? Remember our earlier statement that false religion is based on our desire to be in a place of superiority, able to set everyone's agenda, totally complete and independent in ourselves. The desire to be called a teacher implies that we have superior knowledge. The desire to be called father implies that we have superior maturity. Sadly, none of these titles will satisfy the longing for passionate love.

THE LIFE OF RELIGION

Beginning in Matthew 23:13, Jesus tells the results of buying into a life of religion rather than a life of love.

The Effects of False Religion:
o   Blindness
o   Hiddenness
o   Subversiveness

Blindness: This is a willful blindness that comes because we reject God's definition of reality. We seek to reduce God to our level or try get to Him on our own basis. Our spiritual eyes become clouded and we can't see things as they really are. Only the humble, contrite heart—the heart that trembles at God's word and is obedient to His commands—sees clearly. The key to the knowledge of God is not so much in seeking the knowledge, but rather in obeying what we already have. Disobeying known truth shuts one's eyes to reality as God defines it.

Hiddenness: Jesus said it like this: *"You are like whitewashed tombs, which look beautiful on the outside but on the inside are full of dead men's bones and everything unclean"* (Matthew 23:27). Something about false religion keeps us from opening up and becoming vulnerable. It prevents us from confessing our faults to one another in a discrete manner. It keeps us from allowing people to get close enough to us to speak into our lives. It convinces us that if we are ever going to really make it to this place of "God likeness", we must become independent and all-knowing in ourselves. The tendency toward isolation and independence is always a result of drinking from the fountain of false religion.

Subversiveness: False religion always seeks to manipulate things so that someone's personal agenda can be achieved. For instance, the Pharisees constantly looked for ways to remove anything or anyone that would stop their agenda. Subversiveness takes many forms. However, a good definition is, seeking to control where you have no authority. It is subversion when people who are not in a position of responsibility begin criticizing people who are. People in authority are to be held accountable; but there is a right way to appeal and a wrong way to oppose.

Blindness, hiddenness and subversion are not characteristics of life on the highest level. These qualities produce nothing but a life of misery, dullness and bitterness. False religion makes us actors. We hear so much about the tragedy of Hollywood and how people have become great professionals, have great talents and yet don't know how to live. I'm afraid there is little difference between Hollywood and popular religion. We have taught people how to "act" with an external facade while their lives are falling apart inside. And we have, to a great degree, reduced Christianity to external behavior rather than the internal change of the heart that only comes from a passionate romance with Jesus Christ.

THE CURE

In Revelation chapter 3, we find Jesus, the great lover of our souls, giving us some instructions about how to cure the problem of a cooling, lukewarm love. He says we are to first buy gold *"refined in the fire."* It seems that the trading issue has come up again. You will remember how earlier we talked about repentance in the Kingdom of God always being a trade up. We give up our values and our agenda for His. In this passage, Jesus is saying that we can trade our lukewarmness for His passion if we are willing to acknowledge our need. As long as we pretend that things are okay and try to get by with dull duty, we will continue to live without passion and the excitement that His love brings. To buy gold refined in the fire, is to buy the life of Jesus that has already been through the greatest fire possible. He suffered, died and went through hell for us. Someone may ask, "How can we buy anything from God?" The answer is that heaven's currency is faith. We can receive the grace of God by acknowledging we have nothing to exchange for it but our need. The more we try to overcome apart from faith, the duller our life becomes and the more hopeless it will seem.

There is another aspect of buying gold refined in the fire. I think Jesus is saying to us that we are to value the life that endures. As long as we only value the good feeling experiences and the religious events in life, we will not have adopted His value system. God values the life that perseveres under trial. He is not upset when we stumble and fall. If He has displeasure, it would be at those who refuse to get up and, by faith, trust Him for the strength to go on. Hopefully, one of these days we will stop idolizing the "flash-in-the-pan" personalities and projects that can so easily deceive the populous, and go back to appreciating the life that perseveres over the long haul.

I remember several years ago talking to a friend who had boxed in the same gym with Joe Frasier, the former heavyweight champion of the world. He told me he had asked Mr. Frasier, "Who was the greatest fighter that you knew?" Joe Frasier said, "Without question it was Muhammad Ali. What made him great was that he could take a punch." I thought it was very interesting that most of us who followed the boxing career of Muhammad Ali would have commented about his fancy footwork or his lightening quick left jabs. But one who knew the inside "scoop" knew that what made him great was his ability to persevere even when hurt.

The next thing Jesus encourages us to trade for is *"white clothes."* Obviously, He is referring to a by-faith righteousness. In other words, Jesus is encouraging us to get our focus off our own righteousness and our own self improvement efforts and focus on the reality that we are clothed in His righteousness. Thereby, we have access to His presence continually. To accomplish this, we would have to trade off thoughts of self-accusation and condemnation, as well as honestly believe that we can enter into the presence of God through the shed blood of Jesus. Our access to His unlimited presence does not depend upon anything we do, but depends upon something that has already been done, the shedding of Jesus' blood.

The third thing that Jesus encourages us to trade for is *"eye salve"* to open our blind eyes. We must acknowledge our blindness in order to overcome it. Jesus confronted a blind man in the New Testament and asked him what seemed to be a very curious question, *"What do you want me to do for you?"* The blind man said, *"I want to see"* (Mark 10:46-52). I don't know all that was in Jesus' mind when He asked that question, but I think He wanted the man to publicly confess his blindness so that Jesus could give him his sight.

Paul, in writing to Timothy, tells us that repentance is a grace that is given from God. We must ask for and receive the grace of repentance when we are blind and we need to see from God's perspective. *"Those who oppose him he must gently instruct, in the hope that God will grant them repentance leading them to a knowledge of the truth"* (II Timothy 2:25). Once we think we have figured out all the answers to our questions and solutions to our problems, we immediately become blind to God's perspective. The attitude of humility and repentance keeps our eyes open to see what God is showing us.

The picture we have of Jesus in Revelation chapter 3, is of the lover standing outside the door of His beloved Church, knocking and desiring fellowship. His invitation remains the same; if you hear Him knocking, open the door and let Him in. Could it be as simple as that? Have we have found other lovers and, consciously or unconsciously, shut Jesus out of our love life? It is true that He is a jealous lover. He is not jealous in the way we think of human jealousy, with bitterness and rancor. He is jealous because of His intense desire to give Himself completely to us and for us to give ourselves completely to Him. If we abandon our other lovers and invite Him to come in, Jesus has promised that He will come in and have intimate fellowship with us—individually and with His Church. Someone may ask, "What if I invite Him in and He doesn't come in?" The only answer we can honestly give is that this is a promise from Jesus Himself to His Church; if He is invited in, He will come have fellowship with us.

> *Here I am! I stand at the door and knock. If anyone hears my voice and opens the door, I will come in and eat with him, and he with me.*
> Revelation 3:20

Another wonderful promise Jesus makes to those who will prepare themselves for His knock at the door is in Luke chapter 12. As we acknowledge our need and open the door to Him in humility, we will personally experience the fullness of His unconditional love.

> *Be dressed and ready for service and keep your lamps burning, like men waiting for their master to return from a wedding banquet, so that when he comes and knocks they can immediately open the door for him. It will be good for those servants whose master finds them watching when he comes. I tell you the truth, he will dress himself to serve, will have them recline at the table and will come and wait on them.*
> Luke 12:35-37

CONCLUSION

Too many times we have convinced ourselves that it is possible to live the Christian life apart from passionate love. We tend to reduce it to doctrine, duties, disciplines and denominational emphasis, ultimately finding ourselves crying out in the dryness of our daily experience. Today, because He is a lover, Jesus is knocking at the door of His Church and in the hearts of individual believers. He desires to love us afresh and ignite the passion that is within us, so that all of our activity comes out of passionate love for Him. After all, He said the one thing which would distinguish His disciples from all others would be our love for one another. And we have all discovered that we can't begin to love one another if we are not passionately in love with Him.

So many times, Lord, the initial flame of love dwindles to a flicker. Yet You are a true and faithful lover, longing for the romance to be rekindled. Nothing and no one can satisfy like You, Lord. Warm me with the refining fire of Your love. Ignite my passion anew. In Jesus' Name, Amen.

6 ‖ *PERVERTED LOVE*

We have previously described love as a passion ignited within us when an unmet, sometimes unknown, unspoken need is met by another, causing us to seek union with that source. That source can be legitimate or illegitimate. Therefore, there is the possibility that love can be perverted. This is exactly what happened in the Garden of Eden when man, who was created to love God, sinned and all of his desire was turned inward. Now his passion, which should have been for God only, was turned toward *covetousness, envy, pride* and *wrath. Covetousness* is seeking that which we do not have. *Envy* is not wanting anyone else to have either what we have or don't have. *Pride* is that eternal longing to be in a higher position than we are. And *wrath* is the conflict that comes when others do not live according to our agenda.

Let's first look and see how perverted love gets its foothold. When real love is refused, then illegitimate love takes its place. *"For although they knew God, they neither glorified him as God nor gave thanks to him, but their thinking became futile and their foolish hearts were darkened...Therefore God gave them over in the sinful desires of their hearts to sexual impurity...shameful lust...to a depraved mind, to do what ought not to be done. They have become filled with every kind of wickedness, evil, greed and depravity"* (Romans 1:21-29).

"But why would anyone reject God's love?" someone might object. If we could go back to the Garden of Eden and see Adam and Eve hiding behind a bush we might get a clue. Man in his sinful state is full of shame. Shame prevents us from receiving the unconditional love of God. We are aware that we do not merit it. Our focus is so much on ourselves and our imperfection that we are unwilling to lift our eyes to the Source of life and love.

The history of man could be captured in the picture of Adam and Eve trying to live behind the bush. Their rebellion brought self-conscious shame, so they hid. If they refused the covering God provided, they would be doomed to live behind the bush. All men and women in history who have refused to come out and be covered by God's grace, have found some kind of bush to hide behind. Some hide behind busy activity; some behind the bush of religious activity. Still others find the bush of human intellect. In fact, we have proven reasonably creative at finding our own bush to hide behind.

The fear of being rejected has kept many of us not only from the fullness of human, romantic love but also from the ecstasy of the divine romantic love. For One who is "total perfection" to love the imperfect is hard for us to get into our minds. The gospel of God loving us is too good to be true...but it is.

FALSE LOVERS

In today's relativistic climate there may be different opinions about what perverted love is. Scripture makes it reasonably clear that perverted love is a focus on self. When the Apostle Paul discusses the litany of sins that are a result of our rebellion against God, he lists homosexuality as one of those manifestations. This is a clear example of focusing on self when one gender chooses, for whatever reason, to focus on itself and find its satisfaction within itself. That is the essence of homosexuality. However, many have made the astute observation that the Church itself is suffering from *homosectuality* because we tend not to reach outside of ourselves to embrace that which is different. We want to settle down inside our own sects. Homosexuality is obviously a perverse expression of life, but in reality it is no more selfish than all the other sins listed in Romans chapter 1. They all express a primary focus on self, and they all produce a barren life. This lengthy list includes such selfish manifestations as: envy, murder, strife, deceit, gossip, slander, arrogance, boastfulness, disobedience to authority and so on. All these would be eliminated by the kind of love that focuses on God rather than self.

There are many lovers out there in the world vying for our affection. Prestige and prosperity are walking down every street trying to lure the naive into their clutches. Moralism tries to gather its band of lovers as it seeks to reduce life to living by external principles. Legalism promises a life of fulfillment if we will only follow its rules. There are a myriad of other lovers who promise some sense of pleasure and security if we will only sleep with them. The truth, however, is that the end of the relationship is always bitter.

> *My son, pay attention to my wisdom, listen well to my words of insight, that you may maintain discretion and your lips may preserve knowledge. For the lips of an adulteress drip honey, and her speech is smoother than oil; but in the end she is bitter as gall, sharp as a double edged sword. Her feet go down to death; her steps lead straight to the grave. She gives no thought to the way of life; her paths are crooked, but she knows it not. Now then, my sons, listen to me; do not turn aside from what I say. Keep to a path far from her, do not go near the door of her house, lest you give your best strength to others and your years to one who is cruel, lest strangers feast on your wealth and your toil enrich*

another man's house. At the end of your life you will groan, when your flesh and body are spent. You will say, "How I hated discipline! How my heart spurned correction! I would not obey my teachers or listen to my instructors. I have come to the brink of utter ruin in the midst of the whole assembly."

Proverbs 5:1-14

One of the sure ways we know when we've entered into the field of perverted love is that we have no fruit of joy, peace and glory. The telltale sign is that we constantly focus on ourselves—what we can get, what we can do, what we can become and how the world revolves around us. We will not only try to get our neighbor's agenda to operate with us as its center, but we even try to bend God's agenda to our purpose. Too many who have made a covenant with Jesus are living in spiritual adultery. Our vow was to Him, but when we want to have fun we go to some other source. We give someone or something else our attention, our time, our pleasure, our laughter and our money. When we cease to be extravagant in all these things toward the Lord Jesus, we can be certain that our love has become perverted to some degree.

SUBMITTING TO GOD

How do we get out of this perverted love? James 4:7-10 gives us a great clue. In discussing this very issue James says, *"Submit yourselves then to God. Resist the devil and he will flee from you"* (v 7). What does it mean to submit to God?

- o Trust His Forgiveness
- o Trust Him for His Deliverance
- o Trust Him for His Salvation

Trust His forgiveness: Rather than trying to earn it on our own, we must trust God for our forgiveness. After we have sinned, we can do nothing to make up for that sin but run to Jesus, trusting that God has accepted Jesus' shed blood as completely sufficient to cover that sin forever. God has faith in the blood of Jesus. To submit to Him means we also must place our faith in that same blood. We must not continue with a sense of shame, guilt and self-accusation. That is a denial of the high price Jesus paid to set us free from our own guilt.

> *How much more, then, will the blood of Christ, who through the eternal Spirit offered himself unblemished to God, cleanse our consciences from acts that lead to death, so that we may serve the living God!*
>
> Hebrews 9:14

Trust God for His deliverance: This happens through the cross of Jesus Christ. That's why Paul said to the Corinthians, *"I have chosen to preach nothing among you except Christ and him crucified"* (I Corinthians 2:2). The cross is God's way of delivering us not only from the penalty of sin, through Jesus' payment by His death, but also from ourselves. By faith we can enter into the actual death experience of Jesus. Through the cross we die to ourselves and therefore end being self-obsessed and self-focused. Whatever is wrong with us that was caused by the fall of Adam, can be corrected by our union with Christ through the cross. It is at the cross that we get to start over. We can actually consider ourselves to be dead indeed unto sin but alive to God because of the resurrection of Jesus Christ. I continue to believe that nothing is wrong with us that dying and being resurrected wouldn't fix. The cross is good news to the believer for it means that when we submit to God, by faith in Jesus Christ, we have a new past and a new future. What more could we ask for!

Trust Him for His salvation: We must truly believe that Jesus' life—the same life that Jesus lived while on the earth—has been imparted to us. That being true, we must also believe we are now in the process of being saved by His life-giving presence inside of us because we have been reconciled to God by Christ's death. As we submit by faith to this reality, we can begin to experience the joy, power and freedom that He experienced.

RESIST THE DEVIL

James says after we have submitted to God we can resist the devil.

o   Denounce his authority
o   Declare selfishness your eternal enemy
o   Make "living truth" your treasure

Denounce his authority: Because we have submitted to God, the devil no longer has authority over us. He has no authority to direct our lives, and he has no authority to punish us. Our union with Jesus Christ denies him that right. We may have a battle in our mind over this, but the believer must stand his ground and declare that Satan has no authority in the life submitted to God.

Declare selfishness your eternal enemy: As you know, Satan does not come to us and announce his identity. His work is done through the cover of our own selfishness. We must be alert to the first signs of selfishness, for without a doubt, it is the enemy creeping in to steal our freedom and joy. When selfishness is our enemy and we no longer coddle it and give into it, we have made great strides in resisting the tactics of the enemy.

Make "living truth" your treasure: When the life of Jesus becomes the highest treasure in our life, we will find ourselves spending our resources to gain this treasure. When we focus on life, it is difficult for death to get a foothold. Jesus' life is the *"light of men"* (John 1:4), and light can never be extinguished by darkness. Therefore, as long as we keep our focus on life and light we will find that darkness and death cannot gain a foothold.

CONCLUSION

It is not a shame to have experienced perverted love. It would be a shame, once you realized you have experienced it, to continue in it. God has made a way for us to repent and trade our perverted love for His pure, unconditional, liberating love. Remember, everything Jesus did, He did to set us free. Everything that He is, He is for us—enabling us to enjoy the same fellowship with the Father that He Himself enjoys.

> **Father, sometimes it seems so easy for perverted love to get a foothold in my life. Other "lovers" try to woo me away from You. But because Your sweet love is completely sufficient, Lord, I choose to resist these false lovers and submit only to You. I trust You for forgiveness, deliverance and salvation. I am rich in the treasure of Your "living truth". In Jesus' Name, Amen.**

7 ‖   *OBSTACLES TO INTIMATE LOVE*

Charles was distraught. He had spent several days off from work fasting and praying, yet he felt no deeper intimacy with God. He had tried learning the Greek language so he could properly interpret the New Testament, but that had not produced the kind of fellowship with God for which he hungered. He was involved in every activity of the church hoping the next involvement would bring his desired goal. Now he was at a point of exhaustion. "I don't think God wants to have fellowship with me," he said. Was he right? Is it true that God wants to have fellowship with some of His children and not with all? Does God show favoritism toward the super saints like Noah, Abraham and Enoch, or is the way open for all of us to have intimate fellowship with God?

INTIMACY OR OBSTACLES?

If we believe Scripture, then we have to conclude that God is not hiding from those who want to know Him. He has taken the initiative in coming to us on every occasion. We may sometimes find it difficult during our journey to know more of Him. But we must not lose heart, for the search will produce a hunger in us that will cause us to know Him in a much deeper way when we finally "see" Him. It is true that we cannot know God if He is not willing to show Himself to us. Man's desire alone does not guarantee his knowledge of God, or of anyone for that matter. For instance, we may have a great desire to get to know the President, the Queen, the movie star. But unless that person is willing to give us time, talk to us and reveal himself, we could spend hours in their presence and never really know them. God, however, has given us ample evidence to believe that He wants to know us more than we want to know Him.

> *"Then you will call upon me and come and pray to me, and I will listen to you. You will seek me and find me when you seek me with all your heart. I will be found by you," declares the Lord...*
> Jeremiah 29:12-14a

But if that is true, why do we at times have such a hard time finding that level of intimacy for which we long?

This is not a chapter intent on promoting some severe introspection that leaves us judging our motives and criticizing our efforts. However, when there is a dryness in our soul, it is not a bad idea to do some examination to see if there are some obstacles blocking the revelation that God has so readily given. Isaiah chapter 58 has some wonderful instructions to help us in times like that.

> *For day after day they seek me out; they seem eager to know my ways, as if they were a nation that does what is right and has not forsaken the commands of its God. They ask me for just decisions and seem eager for God to come near them. 'Why have we fasted,' they say, 'and you have not seen it? Why have we humbled ourselves, and you have not noticed?'*
> Isaiah 58:2-3

It seems that the people of Isaiah's day were trying to get God's attention. They wanted God to respond. They wanted their prayers answered. They even said they wanted to know Him intimately, yet God was not responding from heaven and they were confused. God did not leave them in their confusion long. He answered their request by telling them essentially that they had chosen to look for religious keys while neglecting to internalize His laws. They had trusted the act of fasting and religious sacrifice to get God to respond to their request. God was not at all impressed with the kind of fast they had chosen—where they humiliated themselves and practiced self-denial. What He was interested in was their internalizing His own heart.

> *Your fasting ends in quarreling and strife, and in striking each other with wicked fists. You cannot fast as you do today and expect your voice to be heard on high. Is this the kind of fast I have chosen, only a day for a man to humble himself? Is it only for bowing one's head like a reed and for lying on sackcloth and ashes? Is that what you call a fast, a day acceptable to the Lord?*
>
> Isaiah 58:4-5

GOD'S VALUES

Some may argue, "But God's laws are so hard to obey." It is true that man has revealed his inability to please God by living up to external laws. But that is no excuse, because God, according to His New Covenant, has put His law in our hearts. *"This is the covenant I will make with the house of Israel after that time, declares the Lord. I will put my laws in their minds and write them on their hearts"* (Hebrews 8:10). We really don't have an excuse for not obeying the laws of God because they have not only been written in Scripture, they have been written in our hearts. When we choose not to live by these values or follow this guidance, in effect, we stop the flow of God's mercy toward us. The next verses in Isaiah chapter 58 give us a clear word:

> *...Is not this the kind of fasting I have chosen: to loose the chains of injustice and untie the cords of the yoke, to set the oppressed free and break every yoke? Is it not to share your food with the hungry and to provide the poor wanderer with shelter when you see the naked, to clothe him and not to turn away from your own flesh and blood?...*
>
> Isaiah 58:6-7

God reveals something of his internalized laws in these verses:

o   God loves justice and hates injustice
o   God loves freedom and hates oppression
o   God loves generosity and hates selfishness

Any time we give place to injustice, oppression or selfishness we are choosing the opposite of God's heart. It is futile for us to try to use religious keys such as fasting, self-humiliation, self-sacrifice, self-punishment, confession or benevolent deeds to try to get Him to respond when we are neglecting the very essence of His heart.

> *Do not let anyone who delights in false humility and the worship of angels disqualify you for the prize. Such a person goes into great detail about what he has seen, and his unspiritual mind puffs him up with idle notions.*
>
> Colossians 2:18

Why would we neglect *justice, freedom* and *generosity?* We often lack *justice* because we are still addicted to looking out for our own interest. As long as we are our number one priority, we will either consciously or inadvertently treat others with disrespect, and they will end up being the victims of injustice. For instance, in our effort to get the best deal, we can easily justify cheating another out of a fair price for the goods. We complain about the justice system being corrupt as lawyers "get everything

they can" without a sense of fair play. But are we guilty of th
same offense as we unfairly take advantage of others in order t
get the best deal? Do we justify our injustice by such lam
remarks as; "They should have known their product better," o
"It's not my fault if they are desperate or stupid." God was ver
clear in the Old Testament that His people were not to tak
advantage of those in difficult situations, and He has not change
His mind. Leviticus chapter 25 had clear-cut guidelines for th
person who fell on hard times and had to sell some of his propert
There were several ways through which he could ultimatel
redeem that property:

> *...his nearest relative is to come and redeem what
> his countryman has sold...(if) he himself prospers
> and acquires sufficient means to redeem it,...he can
> then go back to his own property. If a man sells a
> house in a walled city, he retains the right of
> redemption a full year after its sale...houses in
> villages without walls around them are to be
> considered as open country. They can be
> redeemed, and they are to be returned in the
> Jubilee. The Levites always have the right to
> redeem their houses...But the pasture land
> belonging to their towns must not sold; it is their
> permanent possession.*
>
> Leviticus 25:25-34

Next, in the area of *freedom*, we believe that in order to b
secure, we must be in control of every situation which woul
sometimes involve other people. Our insecurity leads us t
oppression. The spirit of control does not allow the individual, no
anyone around them, to be free. There is always a kind o
blackmail going on at some level. Wherever there is manipulatio
we can be sure that the liberty of God's Spirit is not there.

In addition, we neglect *generosity* and reveal our poo
stewardship, by trying to collect possessions to make us fe

ecure. After all, we are never sure how much we might need. Only when we have infallible trust in our Father, will we stop ooking out for our own interest and trust Him to provide for us. Then we will be willing to give up control of our own lives in every situation and start giving our lives away.

ELIMINATING OBSTACLES

God, through Isaiah, gave three very practical steps to eliminate the obstacles to intimacy. He said very plainly to do away with oppression and accusation and to help the truly needy. To do away with oppression means to seek liberty as our goal in life, not only our own life, but also everyone with whom we have relationship. To stop accusation means that we take seriously the commands of Scripture to bring our tongue under the control of the Spirit of God. The critical, accusing, gossiping tongue has no place in the life of one who wants intimacy with the Father. To help the truly needy would mean that our focus would be giving rather than getting. God's promise to those who do adopt His heart is breathtaking. He says;

    o   *Your light will break forth like the dawn.*

    o   *Your healing will appear quickly.*

    o   *Righteousness will go before you, and the glory of the Lord will be your rear guard.*

    o   *You will call, and the Lord will answer; you will cry for help, and he will say: Here I am.*

    o   *The Lord will guide you always; he will satisfy your needs in a sun scorched land and will strengthen your frame. You will be like a well-watered garden, like a spring whose waters never fail.*

o   *Your people will rebuild the ancient ruins and will raise up the age-old foundations.*

o   *You will be called Repairer of Broken Walls, Restorer of Streets with Dwellings.*

Isaiah 58:8-9,11-12

What a possibility! What a promise to be claimed if we are willing to follow His practical steps to remove the obstacles that are blocking His flow of mercy.

CONCLUSION

We can be sure that God is not withholding intimacy. He has desired our fellowship since the beginning. He sent His own Son to pay the price for us to have fellowship with Him. If there are obstacles in the way, He has permitted them so that in our hunger we would search for the obstacles and remove them. We may have harbored injustice, oppression and selfishness because it was the only way we knew how to live. But when our hearts get hungry enough for intimacy with the Father, we will be willing to trade our injustice, oppression and selfishness for His justice, freedom and generosity. It won't be a bad trade, and His promise to us is extravagant.

Thank You, Father, that though the journey sometimes seems difficult and dry, You are always there. You do not hide from me, but desire to spend time with me, talk with me and reveal Yourself to me. I don't want to try to open your heart with religious keys. Because I

am Yours, the love flows freely back and forth between us. Thank You for this level of intimacy that is mine. I love You. Amen.

8 ‖ *THE SUCCESS OF THE SECRET LIFE*

Some may read the title of this chapter and think that we've made a typographical error. You might want to suggest that we change it to The Secret of the Successful Life. But I suggest that the title is correct, and, if we really want to know the secret of the successful life, we will want to be successful in the secret life. There is a cry throughout the world from believers who really want to know God intimately. They long to embrace the life of love that has been exhibited in Jesus Christ. Literally thousands are tired of religious duty or lawless living. They have finally decided that, if they are going to be Christians, they are going to embrace the whole thing.

REVEALING THE SECRET LIFE

In Matthew 6:1-18 Jesus identifies three activities that reveal what kind of secret life we have. These activities are *praying, giving*, and *fasting*. In connection with these activities, Jesus makes a promise made no where else in Scripture. He promises an open reward for those who are successful in their secret life. *"... your Father who sees what is done in secret will reward you"*

(Matthew 6:6). Jesus taught that if you give your gifts to the poor so as not to be seen by others, you will be rewarded openly. He said that if you pray in secret without impure motives, you will be rewarded openly. Concerning fasting, Jesus taught His disciples to do it only for the Father to see. Then their reward would be from the Father, not men. Some are praying today to get an open reward. We want the open reward of the anointing of God, the power of God, the favor of God and the blessings of God on our lives. We have looked for these in every religious nook and cranny possible. We have sought them through special religious experiences, unusual revelations and obsessive self-denial. Jesus has again come to our rescue and given us the key to the successful secret life. That key is the word *Father*. Each activity discussed in these verses is always in relationship to and a focus on the Father.

> *When you pray...close the door and pray to your Father who is unseen...Do not be like them, for your Father knows what you need even before you ask him...If you forgive men when they sin against you, your heavenly Father will forgive you...When you it will not be obvious to men that you are fasting, but only to your Father who is unseen; and your Father, who sees what is done in secret, will reward you.*
>
> Matthew 6:5-18

The real key to secret living is focusing on the Father. In John chapters 16 and 17, Jesus made it very clear that His purpose in coming to the earth was to reveal the Father. He told His disciples that their great privilege was to enjoy the Father as He had. He said something so astounding to them that Christians throughout the centuries have had a hard time believing it. Jesus said that we, as His disciples, have the same privilege of union with the Father that He Himself did. He had already made no secret of the fact that every word He spoke was because of His intimate communion with the Father. He said that every deed He did was a response to His Father. He let His disciples know, in every way, that He came to glorify the Father. In John chapter 16, Jesus explained the relationship that the Father offers.

> *...Now is your time of grief, but I will see you again and you will rejoice, and no one will take away your joy. In that day you will no longer ask me anything. I tell you the truth, my Father will give you whatever you ask in my name. Until now you have not asked for anything in my name. Ask and you will receive, and your joy will be complete. Though I have been speaking figuratively, a time is coming when I will no longer use this kind of language but will tell you plainly about my Father. In that day you will ask in my name. I am not saying that I will ask the Father on your behalf.*
> *No, the Father himself loves you because you have loved me and have believed that I came from God.*
>
> John 16:22-27

COMMUNION WITH THE FATHER

It is obvious in these verses that the secret to undefeatable joy is direct communion with the Father. The disciples were going through a time of grief. What caused this time of grief? They were accustomed to having Jesus, the Messiah, as their leader—the one who could heal the sick, raise the dead, cast out demons. He was their security. He was their link with God, and He was about to leave them. They would have no bridge to God when He left. They had put great faith in Jesus' faith and His relationship with the Father. But they had no personal assurance that when Jesus was not there, they would have any kind of favor with God the Father Himself. Until now, the disciples knew they could get Jesus to ask God for anything and they would get it. His faith was valid but they weren't sure about their own. Jesus' response to them was essentially this: "There's coming a time of grief because

I won't be here. But that time of grief will be turned to a time of joy when you realize that you have as much right to fellowship with the Father as I do." It is still true today that when our orphan spirit has been overcome by the spirit of adoption, we understand in our inner man that the Father loves us as much as He loves Jesus Christ. It is also true that we do not have to depend on Jesus' physical presence. We have our own relationship with the Father in His name. When that happens we move into a realm of joy that no man can take away. We understand in our inner man that the union between the believer and the Father is one that cannot be destroyed or even diminished. He is committed to us because we have believed in Jesus Christ. We are as much in covenant with God the Father as is Jesus.

Many people have a terrible misconception of the word father. The actions of our physical fathers have given us some definition of what that word means. Those who have had a dysfunctional father or an abusive father may have pain every time they think of a father concept. However, we must understand that we do not create God in the image of our earthly father. Whether our earthly father was good or evil, we must receive an image of God from the Holy Spirit who reveals to us the true nature of the heavenly Father. Even those who had a good model for an earthly father must have that image changed to the nature of God the Father. No earthly father can adequately represent the heavenly Father that Jesus came to reveal.

Recently, a forty-seven year old man was saying that he had the greatest father who ever lived. He and his father had a wonderful relationship with each other since his earliest remembrance. His father died recently, and he said, "I didn't know how much I had depended upon my earthly father until he was gone, and now I'm having such a greater revelation of my heavenly Father. In this loss, I've been able to see the superiority of the heavenly Father as revealed by Jesus Christ."

Many of us may have misunderstood the relationship of Jesus

and the Father. In my own experience, I perceived that relationship like the relationship between my earthly mother and my earthly father. From my perspective, my father was much more stern than my mom. He didn't seem quite as approachable and he was more absolute in his answers. When my dad said "no", he didn't mean "maybe", and there was no discussion. However, when my mom said "no", I knew she might negotiate. Often times when I needed to communicate something to my father I would tell my mom and she would interpret. And often times she would have to interpret him to me. "Your dad didn't really mean you were the stupidest kid in the whole world," and "He didn't really mean it when he said he was going to snap your neck like a cucumber." I'm exaggerating here, but you get the picture. Many people have told me that they perceive their father and mother in much the same light. It was in this same light that I had interpreted the relationship of God the Father and God the Son. God the Father had, from my early upbringing, seemed to me to be a very severe God. After all, He was the God who spoke to Moses with such terror that the mountains trembled and the people shook in fear. He was the God who allowed the earth to open up and swallow some rebellious people. He seemed to be pretty severe. His "yes" seemed to be an absolute "yes" and His "no" an absolute "no". My picture of Jesus was one who better understood me and who might be able to appease God in some way. Therefore, I felt much more comfortable talking to Jesus than I did talking to God. So it was as if Jesus was the buffer between me and God the Father. The truth is, Jesus is our mediator, but He is not a buffer. Jesus did not come to be a buffer between God and me, but to reveal the very nature of God. It was my misunderstanding of God that caused me to wrongly fear Him. If I want to know the nature of the God of the Old Testament I must know the nature of Jesus Christ

THE MINISTRY OF THE HOLY SPIRIT

When I submit to the ministry of the Holy Spirit this intimate knowledge of God the Father will become mine. It is the ministry of the Holy Spirit to take what Jesus has done and who He is and reveal it to me. This is what the spirit of adoption really is.

It is no secret that the whole world, both Christian and non-Christian, is seeking peace. Only a personal knowledge of the Father will give us peace in the midst of whatever is going on in this world. *"I have told you these things so that in me you may have peace. In this world you will have trouble. But take heart! I have overcome the world"* (John 16:33). What "things" did Jesus tell His disciples so that they would have this kind of peace? I think He was telling them they had direct communion with the Father. This is a lavish promise—that the Father loves us as much as He loves Jesus, and that He is as attentive to our request as He was to that of His only begotten Son. Certainly if we believe that, we could have peace in the midst of every storm. Was that not the secret to Jesus' ability to sleep in the midst of the storm? Was that not the secret to His ability to walk in the midst of a controversy of those who hated Him? He knew He had direct communion with the Father who was in charge of the whole universe. To finally and truly appropriate this promise raises us to a level of living that is far beyond the average. It is a life where we gain specific instruction, guidance and intimacy. It eliminates the unnecessary grief that comes from a sense of being left without external standards, guidance, answers or solutions. We have the privilege of knowing the Father's heart.

Whatever it costs, we must make this trade. We must trade off all our false images of the heavenly Father. If they've come from hurts in our past we must trust the healing grace of God to eliminate them. If they've come from erroneous doctrine they must be erased from our heart. Whatever it takes, we must know the secret of communion with the Father. Jesus paid a high price for us to know the Father as He knows Him. Not to appropriate this wonderful grace is truly a hideous sin.

Jesus said "in that day" we will have a new joy and a new confidence. We will have a new joy because of our confidence in our personal relationship with God the Father. This is that day. Jesus has already paid the price, has already ascended back to heaven, and has sent the Holy Spirit to us. We have no excuse but to appropriate what He has promised.

> *...those who are led by the Spirit of God are sons of God. For you did not receive a spirit that makes you a slave again to fear, but you received the Spirit of sonship. And by him we cry 'Abba, Father.' The Spirit himself testifies with our spirit that we are God's children. Now if we are children, then we are heirs—heirs of God and co–heirs with Christ...*
>
> Romans 8:14-17a

CONCLUSION

To all those who have wrestled time and again with their impure motives, this truth comes as a welcome salvation. Our praying, giving, fasting and all the rest can only be done with pure motives if we are more conscious of our Father than of anyone else, including ourselves. The reality is, if we are not conscious of the Father, we can't help but be conscious of what others think. And if we are conscious of what others think, our motives will inevitably be to impress them, or at least avoid their rejection.

The success of the secret life depends upon our direct communion with the Father. The Holy Spirit has come to make that real in our experience. When we appropriate this truth by faith, then we know the secret of the successful life.

> **What comfort and love surrounds me as You reveal the true meaning of the word, Father. No matter what definition my earthly father gave this word, You gave it true meaning and life. Help me to grasp the depth and magnitude of Your words. I delight in You, knowing You delight in me, my Papa-God. Amen.**

9 ‖ *COMPELLED BY LOVE*

After listening to a lesson on the topic of Christian victory the young man was depressed. The bottom line seemed more like damage control than victory. The practical steps given were reasonable and maybe workable, but they seemed so tedious and full of fear. Essentially he had been told we must refuse any ideas coming into our minds that are from the world. We must also set our purity goals and be accountable to someone to make sure we keep our promises on schedule. Then we are to remind ourselves of the pain of sinful actions. And finally, in order to have victory, we are to make periodic moral and spiritual checkups. "Good idea," he thought. "But is this how Jesus and His boys did it? Where is the inner transformation I hear about?"

VICTORY OR STRUGGLE

Is there really a life of victory for Christians or are we doomed to live a life of restraint and struggle? Is there treasure so valuable that if we find it we will gladly trade everything for it? And is that treasure a life of victory? Could it be possible that the life of love, both promised and demonstrated by Jesus, is available to us if we are willing to buy it?

God was not teasing when He gave us chapters like I Corinthians 13 in Scripture. He meant it when He told us that this life of love is stronger than manipulation and dominion, and more persuasive than political power, physical power or psychological power. He was not painting some fantasy land for us that we could only dream about. He was actually describing the eternal life which He came, not only to model, but to give to those who would trust Him.

Essentially, there are three approaches to the life God offers:

o   Unbelief and independence
o   The life of restraint
o   A life constrained by love

Unbelief and independence: This consists of those who are the "unengaged"; who simply do not believe God offers the best life. They would not mind having His blessings and His rewards, but are unwilling to buy into His whole program. They do not believe that His boundaries were placed there with our good in mind, and they see God's absolutes as prohibitive and oppressive. As a result, they have chosen not to embrace the eternal life Jesus gives those who trust Him.

There are two forms of this approach to life—*lawlessness* and *legalism*. The *lawless* continue to argue silently with God about His right to set boundaries. They still believe the lie Satan announced in the Garden of Eden when he convinced Eve that God was trying to hold something back from His human creations, and that He doesn't have the right to say we can't eat from any tree. This spirit of lawlessness permeates the whole world system and in fact, will be the spirit that motivates the "man of sin" prior to Jesus' second return. *"Don't let anyone deceive you in any way, for that day will not come until the rebellion occurs and the man of lawlessness is revealed, the man doomed to destruction"* (II

Thessalonians 2:3). It is a spirit that affects every aspect of our culture and frequently moves under the cover of religion promoting itself as liberty.

The other form of rejecting the eternal life of Jesus is *legalism*. The legalist has chosen to simply define life in terms of externals. These externals may be goals, standards, rules or expectations. To live as a true legalist, you really don't need a relationship with any person. You only need to know the rules and have a strong will. It is easy to be a legalist if you don't mind living in dryness, deception and defeat. You simply choose the set of standards by which you will judge success and failure, then deny everything else. The truly sad thing about legalism is that the legalist thinks he has life defined and summed up, but in fact has missed it all together while he keeps his rules. He will one day hear the sad words of the Lord Jesus, "Depart from Me, I never knew you."

The life of restraint: This is primarily a life motivated by fear. Actually, it is not a bad first step toward eternal life but it would be sad to live there for very long. At this stage, God is perceived as severe—when His rules are broken or He is personally displeased there is a major penalty to pay. This kind of living expresses itself by suppressing the flesh and restraining behavior. The people who are content to live at this stage must live their lives afraid that at any moment their self-control will fail and they will do something really bad. They protect themselves by building external controls around the laws of God and adding multiple layers of accountability so their sinfulness can be managed. Sadly, their energy and focus is aimed at their flesh rather than at the life of Christ which displaces the flesh life and its desires and behavior. Fear of failure would be a major motivation for those who live with this approach

A HIGHER LEVEL

A life constrained by love: There is a higher level. Rather than living unengaged or restrained by fear, the Christian has the privilege of living a life constrained by love.

> *For Christ's love compels us, because we are convinced that one died for all, and therefore all died. And he died for all, that those who live should no longer live for themselves but for him who died for them and was raised again. So from now on we regard no one from a worldly point of view. Though we once regarded Christ in this way, we do so no longer. Therefore, if anyone is in Christ, he is a new creation; the old has gone, the new has come! All this is from God, who reconciled us to himself through Christ and gave us the ministry of reconciliation: that God was reconciling the world to himself in Christ, not counting men's sins against them. And he has committed to us the message of reconciliation. We are therefore Christ's ambassadors, as though God were making his appeal through us. We implore you on Christ's behalf: Be reconciled to God. God made him who had no sin to be sin for us, so that in him we might become the righteousness of God.*
>
> II Corinthians 5:14-21

The phrase I want to focus on is this, *"For Christ's love compels us."* What a wonderful thought, to be compelled and constrained by love rather than restrained by fear. Wouldn't it be wonderful if the motivating factor in my life was love for Christ, the same love that caused Him to pour out His life for others, that caused Him to live every moment of His existence to please His Father, the life that was free from anxiety, fear, bitterness or wrath. That kind of life surely would be worth selling everything I have to get. It is hard for us as human beings to even imagine being compelled by love instead of fear, selfish ambition, envy or pride. We can't even contemplate living free from our perverted self-consciousness so that the consciousness of our Father is redominant in our thoughts.

This kind of life is possible, but it does not come without cost. costs everything in our life that is contrary to love; the first thing eing our faulty belief system. The fact is, we will ultimately ehave according to what we believe.

I used to have in my bedroom a little plaque that a lady had iven me. It said, "I practice daily what I believe, all else is eligious talk." That little plaque reminded me daily that what I eally believe I will behave. I may try to talk myself into believing ther things but true belief comes out in behavior. If it is true that e are not behaving as those controlled by love, then we are going have to trade some of our old beliefs for new ones that will roduce that kind of life.

We must agree with God's verdict on fallen man.

Life Producing Beliefs

o Fallen man's disease is so severe that
   its only cure is death.

o God valued fallen man so greatly that
   He was willing to die for him.

o Once a man has embraced the cross
   of Jesus Christ, the core motivation of
   his life changes.

"For Christ's love compels us, because we are convinced that ne died for all, and therefore all died" (II Corinthians 5:14). mplicit in this verse is the understanding that God believes that *allen man's disease is so severe that its only cure is death*. This s offensive to our culture because we are still trying to revive allen man and make him work properly. Our culture's popular hilosophy says that man can be fixed apart from dying; that his

problems can be solved through understanding his past and h
psychological or neurological makeup. Social scientists say th
humanity's problems can be solved by improving the environmen
getting rid of injustice and inequality, and teaching people t
conform to behavioral norms. But God's verdict remains th
same; man can't be fixed apart from death—his disease is to
severe. If this is not the case, then God misjudged fallen man ar
actually did a terrible thing when He sent His own Son to die i
order to save man.

BECOMING A NEW CREATION

But there is good news. Jesus came and died in our place s
that, in Him, we could also die. This is not just a metaphor t
speak of Jesus' sacrificial character. By faith we actually ent
into His death and die so that all of our perspective is changed t
our becoming one with Him in His death, burial and resurrectio
You see, God doesn't just want to kill the disease, he wants to sav
the patient. The disease is killed through the cross, but the patie
is saved through the resurrection. The cross of Christ Jesus speak
loudly about two issues. First, it says that man's sin is worse tha
we thought. Secondly, it says that God has taken care of all of th
human dilemma by the death, burial and resurrection of Jesu
Nothing is wrong with man that death and resurrection will n
cure. The wonderful truth is that we can all start over at the cros
This reality is at the heart of this passage. It is what make
possible the statement, *"If anyone is in Christ, he is a ne
creation"* (II Corinthians 5:17). To be a new creation does n
mean an improvement over the old creation. It is a new specie
This kind of transformation requires supernatural power, an
therein lies a problem for the philosophy of this world. Th
supernatural does not "pass the bar" of our reason and ou
scientific investigation. Therefore, much of our culture has troub
believing in the reality of regeneration. If we join with our cultu
and begin to doubt and deny that God still does miracles, then w
have a major problem, because we have a disease that cannot t
fixed apart from the miracle of resurrection. If, in fact, God ha

eased to be a miracle working God, then we cannot be changed. 'he greatest miracle He has ever performed, and continues to erform, is the changing of a fallen man into a redeemed man.

God not only resolved that fallen man must die, but *He valued allen man so greatly that He was willing to die for him*. This elief really is the key to the life of love. Here is the situation: 'allen man was focused on himself, trying to succeed through his wn efforts, filled with fear and anxiety, trying to obtain security hrough his possessions and trying to achieve significance by xalting himself. He lived his life tormented by conflicting lusts nd desires. God looked down and saw all this. Yet He still alued this fallen man and took whatever steps necessary to ossess and restore this treasure. In fact, God valued this ormented man so much that, with joy, He sent His Son to buy the vhole world just so that He could have this precious treasure. 'his is the kind of heart God puts within us when we come to eally embrace the cross of Jesus Christ. We begin to value fallen nan the same way God does. We accept the Father's belief ystem that says, "Fallen man in all of his sin and perversion is till worth dying to save." Those who want a life of peace, power nd prestige, but are unwilling to accept this belief system will ever really have Christian victory. They may opt for Christian nagic; that is, they may try to get God to respond to their requests y pushing religious buttons and seeking to get God to pour His lessings on their own selfishness. This, too, will bring great elusion and depression. Only the life of love is the life of victory.

aution:

Before we trade for this life of love, however, there might be a eed for a word of caution. To accept a belief like this may hange our whole future. Once we start valuing sinful man like iod does, we are going to value reconciliation. The result will nean becoming passionate about sharing the gospel. Our goals nay no longer be to make millions and retire when we are fifty-ine so we can fish all day. We might find ourselves motivated by econciling people with God and even being sacrificial to get it done. It is wise to count the cost before we make the trade.

We must agree with God's view of reconciled man. *"And h*
died for all, that those who live should no longer live fo
themselves but for him who died for them and was raised again
(II Corinthians 5:15). It seems that God actually believes that *onc*
a man has embraced the cross of Jesus Christ the cor
motivation of his life changes. He no longer lives for himself, bu
for the One who died for him. I don't think we really believe tha
about ourselves or our spiritual brothers and sisters. I personall
believe that we do not appeal nearly enough to people's nev
creation identity. We still appeal to men's flesh. For instance, w
will say to believers, "If you trust Jesus He will give you peace
solve your problems and make your life comfortable." Tha
approach still appeals to the fleshly side of man who believes he i
a victim and simply wants to be brought out of his victimization
God has done such a supernatural work in reconciling man to God
that He has changed his basic motivation. We really need t
appeal to each other based on that hope. The reconciled man doe
not want to live for himself, but wants to live for Jesus, who die
for him and was raised again. I believe there are thousands o
Christians who sit in churches every Sunday who are no
challenged at a high enough level. Their challenge is to a life o
comfort rather than to a life of sacrifice. And yet in their inne
man they are crying out to give their lives away for the One wh
died for them. A true Christian will never be satisfied until h
lives his life wholly to please someone else—and that someon
else can only by God. Anyone who lives with a focus on self—hi
problems, needs and desires—will live miserably. You can be sur
of it. None of us will ever have life at its best until we ar
expressing the nature of our *new species* character. One of th
laws of created order is that species determines behavior. Dog
bark because that is their species. Cats meow because they are o
a different species. Unredeemed sinners live for themselve
because that is the nature of the species. But reconciled man ha
in his innermost being a desire to live for the One who died fo
him.

CONCLUSION

There is a life of victory for the Christian. It is the life of love promised and demonstrated by Jesus. It is His life of love that compels and constrains us rather than fear restraining us. What beliefs have to change if our behavior is going to express the life of love? We must agree with God's verdict on fallen man: *fallen man must die.* We must agree with God's value of sinful man: *sinful man is worth dying for.* We must agree with God's view of reconciled man: *reconciled man's innermost being wants to please the One who died for him.*

> **Thank You, Father, that You have given me the privilege of living a life compelled and constrained by love—Christ's love. Thank You that I wasn't just "patched up", but that my old life died. You made me a completely new creation—what a miracle of love. I want to share this love with You and with others for Your sake, Lord. In Jesus' Name, Amen**

10 ▌ *IGNITING THE PASSION FOR LIFE*

What is the evidence of a passion which has been ignited and a life compelled by love? How do you tell when someone is living with love constraining them rather than fear restraining them? First, it is a life that lives only to please God. *"So we make it our goal to please him, whether we are at home in the body or away from it"* (II Corinthians 5:9). In reality, the whole letter of II Corinthians is written to describe the uniqueness of the life compelled by love as opposed to the life that has not been united with Christ. In this letter, Paul had previously discussed with the Corinthians how God sovereignly led them through trouble so that, **in** the trouble, they could experience the comfort of the Holy Spirit. They experienced His comfort so they would then give that same comfort to others who were walking in trouble. He also explained to them (in chapters 2 and 3) the unique nature of the New Covenant life as opposed to the Old Covenant life. He explained that it is an internal operation rather than external, and that we as believers have the privilege of being the body through which the Holy Spirit expresses the life of God. In chapter 4, he speaks to them of the *privilege* of suffering in the presence of unbelievers enabling them to see the life and light which reflects from deep within our hearts once our human vessel is broken. In this context, we learn that whoever lives his life to please God, has first been convinced that nothing in this temporal world will ever totally satisfy.

> *Now we know that if the earthly tent we live in is destroyed, we have a building from God, an eternal house in heaven, not built by human hands. Meanwhile we groan, longing to be clothed with our heavenly dwelling, because when we are clothed, we will not be found naked. For while we are in this tent, we groan and are burdened, because we do not wish to be unclothed but to be clothed with our heavenly dwelling, so that what is mortal may be swallowed up by life. Now it is God who has made us for this very purpose and has given us the Spirit as a deposit, guaranteeing what is to come.*
>
> II Corinthians 5:1-5

Paul speaks openly here about the longing inside of us that cannot be satisfied by anything in this world. Neither money, position, influence nor power can meet the need inside us which can only be satisfied by another *world*. Someone has aptly said, "We are trying to make this world a full meal when God only intended it to be an appetizer." This longing inside us is part of our new species creation. It is a part of what happens when we go through the death, burial and resurrection with Jesus Christ. We come out of the world with a longing for an unhindered, undistracted fellowship with God the Father. We are not so much into streets of gold and clouds to lay down upon, but we have a genuine longing for eternal realities.

In Psalm 84, we find an Old Testament saint who has tasted this same eternal longing. *"How lovely is your dwelling place, O Lord Almighty! My soul yearns, even faints for the courts of the Lord; my heart and my flesh cry out for the living God"* (Psalm

84:1-2). This is a portrait of a person who has experienced the "eternalness" of Jesus Christ. There is something inside this saint that is longing—deeply yearning—to live in God's house. Once man has truly tasted the goodness of God, it awakens a desire to know more and more of Him. This should not be surprising. Why would any man fear living in the presence of Someone who is totally good and completely powerful? He can't do anything bad because He has nothing bad in His heart. He does good because that is His nature.

"Blessed are those that dwell in your house; they are ever praising you" (Psalm 84:4). This would be a common characteristic of those who live in God's unhindered presence. When we go to the book of The Revelation and see how things are going on in the heavens, we see that every creature there is, in some form, continually praising God.

"Blessed are those whose strength is in you, who have set their hearts on pilgrimage" (Psalm 84:5). The Psalmist is essentially saying, "Blessed are those who are committed to the journey of knowing all there is to know of God. Blessed are those who have this yearning in their heart. They are willing to walk through whatever it takes to know and embrace this life of God." Evidently, something about this life of love, when embraced, causes one to throw unnecessary caution to the wind and to venture out into the uncharted waters of life. The fear of disappointment, failure and even death is not enough to stop the one whose heart has embraced the very heart of God. This heart has been ignited with passion.

"As they pass through the Valley of Baca (weeping)*, they make it a place of springs"* (Psalm 84:6). What a beautiful description of those who have this taste of eternity on their lips. Wherever they go they turn bitterness and suffering into a valley of springs. They don't spend much time complaining toward God about the difficult paths. they can testify, "I want God more than I want comfort."

We see in this Old Testament Psalm, a beautiful description of the life that has been ignited by love—a life that longs for the eternal; that lives only to please God and realizes that nothing in this world can completely satisfy the deepest longings of the heart. someone recently commented on the level of commitment in the average American Christian, "There just doesn't seem to be any willingness to sacrifice." Maybe the reason for this is that there is nothing in this world worthy of this kind of sacrifice. And if our focus is on the temporal things of this world, we really have not found anything worth selling it all for.

HOW DO WE JUDGE

Another major evidence of being compelled by love, is the ability and proclivity to regard no man simply after the flesh. *"So from now on we regard no one from a worldly point of view. Though we once regarded Christ in this way, we do so no longer"* (Corinthians 5:16). To judge from a worldly point of view means to judge without benefit of divine revelation. It doesn't always mean that we are judging sinfully, but it does mean that we are judging with limitations. We are only judging on evidence gained apart from revelation. The Apostle Paul used Jesus Christ as an example of the two ways of knowing someone. First, Paul (then known as Saul) knew Jesus after the flesh. He judged that Jesus was an illegitimate child—reason and rumor indicated that. The fact is, Jesus' mother was not married at his conception, and Jesus Himself made it clear that Joseph as not His ultimate father. Judging on apparent facts, you would have joined Paul in judging that Jesus was illegitimate. Paul also believed that Jesus was the leader of a cult. Jesus taught a system of truth that was contrary to the popular teaching of the tradition and leaders of that day. Jesus was judged as a seditionist (one who incites rebellion to authority) and a cult leader. Paul believed this so strongly, that he was committed to the extinction of Jesus and all of His followers. Paul deeply believed he was doing God a favor by getting rid of all these heretics. He also believed that Jesus was a criminal. After all, He was crucified outside the gates of the city in the place of the criminal and died the death of a convicted prisoner. Paul had heard the testimony of the disciples that Jesus had been raised from the grave, but because that did not fit in with his world view, he had rejected that story and perceived the disciples as liars.

What difference a little revelation on the road to Damascus made for Paul. After he encountered Jesus by revelation, he had a whole new way of evaluating things. When his eyes were opened, he saw that Jesus was truly the Lord of the universe and gladly submitted to Him. At that point he began to judge Jesus differently and knew Him in the Spirit. Now Paul had revelation to reinterpret all his facts.

We must not lose this truth. If we do not take advantage of revelation, we will find ourselves judging according to a worldly point of view. One of the reasons there is so much disunity in the body of Christ is because we have not been willing to learn how to discern each other in the spirit. We often become critical and judgmental because we are judging on the basis of the apparent and not with the aid of God's perspective. God views every reconciled man and woman as a new creation. His concern is with their destiny, not so much their history. His desire is to encourage their inner man to become strong so that He displaces the effects of the outer man that was trained by the god of this world. When God's perspective becomes precious to us, we too will find ourselves speaking words of encouragement and edification rather than words of condemnation and criticism. It is possible and essential for us to know each other in the spirit. We do not have a right to look at another Christian brother or sister apart from remembering that they are a new creation made that way by the very word of God. He or she is not to be defined by behavior, denominational affiliation, natural family, biological makeup, skin color or sex. None of these truly define a Christian. A true believer is defined by the reality of being a new creation with a longing to know eternal God. This believer has a destiny to live his life for others and to ultimately glorify God. His sins are forgiven, he is reconciled to God and he is of great value. If he is viewed in any other way, he is being misjudged.

RECONCILIATION

There is one more characteristic of a life of love. It will be a life committed to reconciliation. The love-controlled Christian believes reconciliation will finally solve man's basic problem. He believes that when man, who has been hostile toward God, is reconciled to God through Jesus Christ, his own hostility will be taken away. Man will be back in the presence of God enjoying the life of God and living with the core of his being to please God. Those who really believe this have an uncommon boldness and an almost frightening simplicity. They are not afraid to get into the mix of humanity and declare their message. It is not a solution they found in a science laboratory or in a philosophy discussion, but in an encounter with God that changed the very core of their being. With absolute confidence they can say to men and women of every nation, *"God was in Christ reconciling the world to himself"* (II Corinthians 5:19). They know what is wrong with man and they know God's solution. It is not theory nor formula. It is a life—a life worth selling everything to get. And that life, once embraced, makes you want to give it away.

CONCLUSION

What have we said about the evidences of this life ignited by passionate love? It is a life that lives to please God. The focus has been taken off of self-satisfaction and placed on God's pleasure. It also refuses to judge only after the flesh and chooses to judge after the spirit. What will it be for us? Are we willing to venture out and embrace a life of love? That love caused God to send His Son to the world. It caused Jesus to put His life on a cross, and it caused twelve disciples to give their lives in sacrifice so that the light within them could be expressed through their broken bodies. We all agree that we would love peace—the absence of strife—on the inside. The question remains, "Are we willing to buy the whole field (the whole life of love) in order to get the treasure?" God has made the offer. It is time to step up, make the trade and ignite the passion for real life.

It is true, Lord, that nothing and no one can satisfy the longings of my heart but You. Your treasure far exceeds anything the world can offer. You have reconciled me to Yourself, and I embrace Your life of love. You are my passion, Lord. In Jesus' Name, Amen

Other Books By Dudley Hall

Jesus is preparing new wineskins for the new wine He is pouring throughout His Church. This book helps you confront the fears and lessens the pain from coming "out of the comfort zone."

$9.00

If you are tired of struggling, feeling guilty and never measuring up, let the message of grace breathe life back into you. Step out of the complexities of religion into a simple but passionate love relationship with God.

$11.00

Christian Maturity Series

Life on the highest plane requires an energy that is only released when love is ignited. Passionless living will never produce holiness nor liberty. However, life with passion will bring a fullness that liberates and satisfies.

$7.00

Christian growth is the process of "trading up." When there is a treasure to be found, even the search can be exhilarating. God has offered a life worth the search if you know where to look and how to trade up to obtain it.

$7.00

Prayer is not only the opportunity to fellowship with God, but a partnership with Him. As we send up prayer (incense), He answers back with expressions of His power (thunder). When we engage on prayer from this perspective, we experience heaven affecting earth.

$7.00

Books By T.D. Hall

This study guide is an excellent tool to help strengthen believers— especially new converts—about things that are truly ours as Christians.

$5.00

Biblical encouragement and information to help us develop and express the love of Jesus Christ to one another.

$4.00

Dudley Hall's Monthly Message

Have you heard about . . .

Dudley Hall has a uniquely refreshing ministry of grace and restoration. "He makes the essential things seem simple" is a common remark from one who has heard Dudley speak. If you want a no-nonsense approach to living, you will benefit from these messages. While you laugh and sometimes cry, truth will grip you in such a practical way that you are encouraged to put it into practice.

From a background of religion substituted for life, Dudley shares a message of grace and simplicity. Liberation from legalism as well as total involvement in the Kingdom of God give balance to a message designed to fulfill our destiny in Christ.

Literally thousands have been deeply touched. Many have been receiving monthly tapes and outlines for years. They have found a trustworthy resource and value it.

This is not just a program of random messages selected to impress people or promote sales. It is a "life in process" being shared through a craftsman's skill and disciple's heart. We hope you try it, we think you'll like it!

SCLM ORDER FORM

MAIL ORDER TO:
SCLM, PO BOX 101, EULESS TX 76039
SEE CHART FOR SHIPPING & HANDLING CHARGES

NAME _____

ADDRESS_____

CITY_____ST_____ZIP_____

PHONE_____

VISA/MASTER CARD ORDERS: CALL 1-800-530-4933
MONDAY-FRIDAY, 8:00 A.M. TO 5:00 P.M. (CST)
$10 MINIMUM ORDER REQUIRED ON CHARGES
PLEASE CHARGE TO MY VISA/MASTER CARD:

NO._____EXP. DATE _____

SIGNATURE_____

AVAILABILITY & PRICES SUBJECT TO CHANGE WITHOUT NOTICE.
ONLY U.S. CURRENCY ACCEPTED FOR PAYMENT.
ALLOW 4 TO 6 WEEKS FOR DELIVERY.

#	ITEM	EA	TOTAL